DR. SCHUBINER IS A COMPASSIONATE AND DEVOTED PHYSICIAN whose unique approach has helped hundreds of people—including many of my own patients—heal their pain and reclaim their lives. This book will give thousands more access to this revolutionary program.

—Michael C. Hsu, MD, Physical Medicine and Musculoskeletal
Specialist, Kaiser-Northwest Permanente, Portland, Oregon

HOWARD SCHUBINER'S WORK is a tremendous advancement in the field of pain relief. His visionary thinking and comprehensive program will heal untold numbers of chronic pain patients. The book should be required reading for all patients and physicians who deal with chronic pain.

—John Stracks, MD, Department of Family Medicine, Integrative
Medicine Program, Northwestern University, Chicago, Illinois

UNLEARN YOUR PAIN EXPLAINS THE SCIENCE behind chronic pain in a common sense way that everyone will understand. Dr. Schubiner's revolutionary program is based upon his groundbreaking research and really works. This book is the answer to your long search for the cure to your pain.

—Steven Gurgevich, Ph.D., Clinical Assistant Professor of Medicine,
Arizona Center for Integrative Medicine, University of Arizona
College of Medicine

I HAVE SUFFERED FROM PAIN since I was a teenager. I have been diagnosed with more disorders than I could name. But no one was ever sure what was really wrong. Dr. Schubiner's course saved my life. Thank God I now realize that I have Mind Body Syndrome.

      —Walter Lanier, Anderson, South Carolina

PHYSICAL THERAPY, CORTISONE INJECTIONS, and chiropractic treatment didn't help the intense pain in my back and down my leg. Over a year, I spent thousands of dollars without relief. Three weeks after I started Dr. Schubiner's program, the pain was gone. I am still amazed that it worked, and I cannot be more grateful.

      —Gwen Clark, New Baltimore, Michigan

THIS PROGRAM TAUGHT ME that my life experiences had caused my pain. The exercises brought about incredible insights, and the words flowed out of my head and onto the paper. A huge weight had been lifted, and consequently my back pain is gone.

      —Denise Marsh, Royal Oak, Michigan

AS A HEALTH CARE PROVIDER, I was skeptical when I heard about Mind Body Syndrome. Thanks to Dr. Schubiner, I now understand the connection between my emotional state and my physical pain. His program gave me techniques that I have used to control my symptoms and reclaim my life. Thank you so much, Dr. Schubiner.

      —Diane Olsem, RN, Brighton Township, Michigan

DR. SCHUBINER'S MIND BODY SYNDROME PROGRAM enabled me to free myself from fibromyalgia pain which was basically running my life for thirteen years. I am finally on the road to recovery and feel so much more in control of my life and my health.

      —Cindy Corey, Livonia, Michigan

I USED DR. SCHUBINER'S COURSE after everything else failed to stop chronic hamstring pain. His course told me exactly what to do and what not to do, on a daily basis. It took me about two months, but I am now able to walk, work out at the gym, and I now don't worry about my every move.

      Steve Hansen, Easton, Maryland

DR. SCHUBINER'S MIND BODY PROGRAM TAUGHT ME that I have control over my back pain. I quit worrying about all the "physical" problems that I had been told were wrong with my neck and back and started to concentrate on what was going on in my mind. When I realized how much pain had become my identity, I began to heal. Where I could only see a lifetime of pain, I have now regained a healthy and active life.

      —Cathy Gibson, Northville, Michigan

I WAS A FIBROMYALGIA SUFFERER for over twenty-five years, and despite excellent medical care, my severe pain persisted. Dr. Schubiner's program helped me uncover the root causes of my pain and gave me the tools to deal with it. *Unlearn Your Pain* is a truly astounding program. Within the first week, I could not believe how much the pain decreased and my energy levels increased. I continue to be pain free because *Unlearn Your Pain* is now my recipe for living.

—*Fran Baiamonte, Burlington, Connecticut*

I WAS DIAGNOSED WITH TWO HERNIATED DISCS and a pinched nerve as a result of my auto accident. I tried every medical treatment from physical therapy to injections to heavy narcotics. The cycle of pain and suffering continued for three-and-a-half years. It wasn't until I took Dr. Schubiner's Mind Body program that my pain subsided.

—*Marnina Sullivan, Detroit, Michigan*

AFTER SUFFERING WITH SEVERE HAND PAIN for more than three years and not getting any relief from more than eight doctors plus several alternative healers, I had begun to lose hope of ever recovering. Dr. Schubiner's program explained my pain in a way that made perfect sense, and after completing the program, I can honestly say that my pain is virtually gone. In addition, I now understand myself much better, and this has made me a better person.

—*Edward Samuels, Chicago, Illinois*

AT A TIME WHEN I THOUGHT I WAS OUT OF OPTIONS to deal with severe bladder and pelvic pain, Dr. Schubiner's program gave me the tools to take control of my life and manage my symptoms. All other traditional treatments had failed. I am forever grateful, and I continue to employ these techniques in many aspects of my life.

—*Erica El-Alayli, Brighton, Michigan*

AFTER SEVEN YEARS OF SEVERE BACK PAIN which no doctor, drugs, physiotherapist, chiropractor, acupuncturist, or massage therapist could fix, this program gave me relief within a couple of months. The techniques are easy to use, have given me great insight, and, best of all, relieved my pain. I recommend it highly — it changed my life!

—*Lisa Manchester, London, UK*

DR. SCHUBINER'S PROGRAM NOT ONLY HELPED ME break a cycle of nearly continuous headache, it provided me with a broader, deeper, and very useful understanding of how psychological and emotional issues impact my physical well-being.

—*Eric Keller, Ferndale, Michigan*

unlearn your pain

Printer: Sheridan Books, Inc.

CD Replication: Kopy-Rite

Printed in the United States of America.

Cover Photograph: Getty Images, Photodisc

Author Photograph: Rob Vinson

Design and Layout: Eric Keller

Set in Trade Gothic and ITC Century.

Schubiner, Howard with Betzold, Michael

Unlearn Your Pain: a 28-day process to reprogram your brain

ISBN-13: 978-0-9843367-0-8

ISBN-10: 0-9843367-0-2

Howard Schubiner, MD

www.unlearnyourpain.com

unlearn your pain

A 28-DAY PROCESS TO REPROGRAM YOUR BRAIN

**By Howard Schubiner, MD,
with Michael Betzold**

MIND ✳ BODY
PUBLISHING

To my wonderful parents, Lorraine and Elliot I. Schubiner

May you have the commitment
To heal what has hurt you,
To allow it to come close to you,
And, in the end, become one with you.
— Gaelic blessing

table of contents

preface

My mentor in medical school was Dr. Muir Clapper, a very wise and aging physician, who knew that I was the kind of person who wanted to challenge the status quo. He told me, "Howard, get your tickets." He meant that, if I wanted to shake things up in medicine, I should get good training to develop the expertise I would need. I listened to his advice.

Since I graduated from medical school in 1978, I have become board certified in Internal Medicine, Pediatrics, and Adolescent Medicine. I spent most of my career at Wayne State University Medical School in Detroit and became a full Professor there in 2002. I have conducted research studies, taught medical students and residents, authored articles in medical journals, and practiced medicine for thirty-two years. I participated in the creation of a holistic medical center, and I studied acupuncture in China. I have also been listed on the Best Doctors in America list on several occasions. I got my tickets, but what was I to do with them?

In 2003, my boss and friend at Providence Hospital in the Detroit area, Dr. Ernie Yoder, told me about a patient of his who had a remarkable recovery from severe back and hip pain. He suggested that I take a look at the book that helped her become pain free within a few weeks. She had read *The Mindbody Prescription* by Dr. John Sarno, a rehabilitation physician at New York University. Almost forty years ago, Dr. Sarno realized that pain was a relatively common manifestation of stress and emotional reactions to stress. He became a pioneer in the field of mind body medicine and has helped innumerable people through his work and his writing. Yet only a relatively small number of physicians have incorporated this work into their practices. In fact, few physicians are even aware that syndromes such as back and neck pain, headaches, fatigue, fibromyalgia, temporo-mandibular joint syndrome, and irritable bowel and bladder syndromes can be caused by stress due to unresolved emotions.

When I looked back on my own life, I realized that I too had experienced physical symptoms in response to stress and emotions. My neck began to hurt in 1983 and has caused me significant disability over the years. I've had headaches, diarrhea, and back pain from time to time as well. Now that I am fully aware of the incredible connection between the mind and the body, I am almost always able to get rid of the aches and pains that arise by recognizing them for what they are: physical symptoms as a manifestation of stress, worry, anxiety, fears, anger, and the many other emotions that come with being human.

In 2003, I started the Mind Body Medicine program at Providence Hospital in Southfield, Michigan. I have worked extremely hard to find innovative exercises and approaches to help my patients. I have also learned a tremendous amount from my patients. They have shown great courage in the face of severe pain and adversity, and they have helped me to expand the program and make it better.

Two significant things usually occur in people who enter the Mind Body Medicine program. First, their physical symptoms improve. This is the case for the majority of patients within the first month of taking the program. Many others improve later, though not all patients have gotten rid of all of their symptoms. The second thing that typically occurs is that most people learn to understand themselves much better. They learn what issues in their life have the greatest impact on them and why. They begin to see that issues from their childhood often influence their response to issues occurring in the present. And most importantly, they learn techniques for dealing with the issues most relevant to them in both the past and present. In short, they begin to achieve mastery and a sense of control over their emotions, their reactions to stress, and most importantly, their own bodies. I have found that even those people whose physical symptoms do not improve are still grateful for the program because it helps them learn so much about themselves.

Because of these gratifying results in my work, I have decided to write this book so more people can have access to the program that my patients have found so beneficial. I am also writing this book to educate physicians about Mind Body Syndrome. Modern medicine has made many advances for heart disease and cancer. However, for the millions of people with Mind Body Syndrome, medical advances have not been helpful and are actually a part of the problem. To really help people with these syndromes, we need to change medicine by educating both the public and physicians to recognize and treat these disorders more effectively, which can eliminate a great deal of needless suffering.

To your health,

Howard Schubiner, MD

Southfield, Michigan

February 2010

acknowledgments

I am fortunate to have many people to thank. I wanted to write this book for a few years but did not start because the task seemed too overwhelming to undertake on top of my other responsibilities. My good friend, Michael Betzold, an excellent writer, gave me both the encouragement and the resources (his fine writing and editing skills) to complete this project. Another friend, Maureen Dunphy, who designed the course "Journaling as Writing Tool" at Oakland University, provided me with resources about and contributed the initial design of several writing exercises.

I wouldn't have known about the underlying cause of chronic pain without an interaction with a longtime friend, colleague, and former supervisor, Dr. Ernest Yoder. Ernie set me on this course with a single conversation and then allowed me to develop a new line of practice and research within our hospital. Dr. John Sarno is a pioneer and visionary who had the insight and courage to find a new way to understand back pain almost forty years ago. I hope that I can help to expand upon his work and bring it into the mainstream of medical practice.

The work of several scientists and authors has been extremely influential, and I'd like to thank them for their cutting-edge work. Drs. Daniel Wegner, Timothy J. Wilson, and Joseph LeDoux wrote books that opened my mind to some of the science behind Mind Body Syndrome (see Appendix). My mindfulness meditation teachers, Jon Kabat-Zinn, Saki Santorelli, Melissa Blacker, Ferris Urbanowski, and Elaine Greenberg, taught me the skills that have helped me infuse this program with the thought and practices of mindfulness.

I have been fortunate to be able to work with several excellent researchers and thinkers, such as Drs. Dan Clauw and Dave Williams from the University of Michigan. Dr. Mark Lumley from Wayne State University has been an invaluable asset in furthering a research agenda and acting as a sounding board for new ideas. Dr. Michael Hsu worked tirelessly with me on the fibromyalgia research study and helped me sharpen my concepts. Dr. John Stracks has been a great source of support and the co-organizer of our first Mind Body professional meeting.

I would like to express my gratitude to Eric Keller and Rob Vinson, who are not only good friends but very talented in their fields of graphic design and photography/videography, respectively. I thank one of my oldest friends, Mike Blumenthal, who is now also my website designer and advisor. I am very grateful to my daughter, Lindsay, for her editing skills and to my brother-in-law, George Nolte, for his expert proofreading. And I acknowledge my men's group, the intrepid Council of Men, who have supported and challenged me for twenty years.

The people who seek my help and entrust their lives and their stories to me are the reason I keep doing this work. (The names of several patients in this book have been altered to protect their identities.) They are inspirational in their courage to stand up for themselves and, often, to the medical profession. They teach me new things every day about the mind and the body, and they help me to be a better doctor and person.

I thank my children, Lindsay and Gabe, who have taught me many things and who give my life great meaning. My parents have given me incredible love and support every day of my life, and I owe everything to them. Finally, my wife and best friend of twenty-six years, Val Overholt, allows me to think I'm brilliant and laughs at my foibles. On a daily basis, she provides me with what one of my wise ancestors suggested is necessary to be content and balanced: keeping a piece of paper in one pocket which reads, "For my sake the world was created," and in the other pocket, "I am but dust and ashes."

chapter 1
The Truth About Your Pain

Telling people about Mind Body Syndrome is like telling them
that the earth is round, when they KNOW that it's flat!
— Anonymous patient

Vitiant artus aegrae contagia mentis.
(When the mind is ill at ease, the body is affected.) — Ovid

It hurts.

Your pain is awful. Your misery is unrelenting. No matter what you do, you can't get rid of it.

You went to your doctor, and he told you that you had a medical condition: degenerative disc disease, spinal stenosis, fibromyalgia, irritable bowel syndrome, whiplash, or something else. Your doctor prescribed drugs. You took them, but they didn't really help. Maybe you even had surgery, but that didn't stop the pain, whether it was in your back, your head, your neck, your gut, or all over.

Perhaps you have explored alternative medicine. Maybe you took herbal remedies, had therapeutic massages, or saw a chiropractor. You're considering acupuncture, hypnosis, and even crystals, if that might help. Some of these treatments may have provided temporary or partial relief, but still the pain is there, day after day after day. You've gone to so many health practitioners that you are starting to feel no one can help you because no one understands the real problem. Maybe your doctor even referred you to a psychiatrist or psychologist, suggesting that your pain isn't real—that it's all in your head.

But you know you're not imagining your pain. You're not faking it to gain attention or sympathy. It's about time someone in the medical profession recognized that the pain in your body is real. It's about time that someone in the medical profession told you that there is a reason for your pain and a way to cure it.

I am that doctor, and I'm telling you: Your pain is real, there is a reason for it, and there is a cure for it. The only way to relieve the pain is to find the underlying cause of it, to get to the bottom of it. The problem is not in your head. It's in your diagnosis.

Some doctors may say you have a serious medical condition, but if they don't know how to cure it, their diagnosis doesn't help you. Perhaps alternative health practitioners will tell you that your spine is not properly aligned or your aura is out of whack or your chi is diminished. All of these are different ways of looking at your body, but none of them will succeed if they're not correctly diagnosing why your body hurts.

I have some good news for you. Unless you have a medical problem resulting in clear pathology in your body (which can be determined by routine medical tests), your pain can be cured. Following this program, you can take some relatively easy steps to vanquish it.

Like tens of millions of Americans and countless others around the globe who suffer from chronic back pain, muscle pain, headaches, migraines, stomach pain, and other misdiagnosed conditions, you're hurting because of overly sensitized nerve connections between the brain and the body. These connections have created a vicious cycle of pain that can last for months, years, or even decades unless you do what it takes to stop it. This cycle of pain signals has been "learned" by your nervous system—and the longer these signals keep firing, the more sensitized and overactive the nerves become, and the more pain you feel.

The event that started this horrible pain cycle could have been an injury or a stressful event in your life, or it could have come out of the blue. A very careful and detailed look at your current situation and your life history will reveal how your brain is amplifying this pain and perpetuating the vicious cycle.

The best news is that you don't have to live the rest of your life with this pain. Whether you've had it for a few weeks or for many years, it can be beaten. Just as your nervous system has learned to make your body hurt, you can use your brain to unlearn the pain. There's a way to retrain your brain so that your body isn't contorted into pain. This book will explain how this can be done without drugs or surgery, by anyone with the motivation to do so.

In fact, if you begin to understand this syndrome and recognize what causes it, you've already taken a powerful first step. And the rest of the steps, though they require wholehearted commitment, are not difficult. They are all explained in this book, and the whole program is laid out for you to work through. Improvement may occur within days or weeks, even if you've been suffering for a long time. And by doing the program you can get more than temporary or partial relief. You can achieve complete freedom from the pain and distress that have hobbled you.

Starting today, you can break the connection between your nervous system and your physical pain. And you can start to use your mental energy to overcome your limitations and rebuild your life.

I know this is true because I have done it myself. I've changed my understanding of the source of my pain, and I can now prevent the stresses of everyday life from producing pain in my body. More importantly, I've seen the same transformation in hundreds of my patients.

This program is not risky or far out. It doesn't require belief in an alternative paradigm of medicine or philosophy. The work of unlearning your pain is based on solid science and common sense.

The Pathways of Pain

Pain begins when nerve pathways from the brain to the body are stimulated or "fired." Over time, these pathways can become "wired" into the brain's circuitry. The nervous system learns to create chronic pain, even though there is no serious medical condition in the body, and even though any injury that may have precipitated the pain has long ago healed.

Everyone knows that if you break your arm, it will hurt, but after the fracture heals in a few weeks, the pain will disappear. But I have seen hundreds of people whose pain began with an injury but lasted five, ten, even twenty years. Why? The body has surely healed. The answer to this puzzle is found in the connections between the brain and the body.

Many people have heard about "phantom limb" pain, the pain that is felt in the area of an arm or a leg that has been amputated. There is clearly nothing wrong with that area—it isn't even there—yet this pain can be severe. We now know that this pain is caused by sensitized nerve connections and the creation of nerve pathways in the brain.

The good news is that the brain and the nervous system can be retrained to get out of the ruts that produce pain and to forge new nerve pathways to freedom from pain. An increasing body of evidence is showing that the brain has amazing neuroplasticity—it is always learning and creating new structural pathways. All you have to do is tap into that power and use it to reprogram your response to pain and to the factors that intensify that pain.

There are three major components of the nervous system that create the vicious cycle of pain: the nerves that send pain signals from the body to the brain; the brain itself, where those nerve signals are interpreted; and the nerves that send signals back to the body. The best way to end chronic pain and other chronic symptoms is by retraining the brain, the controller of the nervous system. Most people don't realize that the brain can both create and cure chronic painful conditions, so they search for cures by using drugs or surgery that try to cover up the pain. Cutting-edge brain research demonstrates that it is possible to change the brain pathways and interrupt this vicious cycle.

Stress and Pain

Pain cannot be felt without the brain, which interprets nerve signals and transforms them into the experience of pain. Of course, it is important to be able to feel pain so we can protect ourselves from danger. However, these pathways often tend to get reinforced over time by our reactions to the pain. Just about everyone who has chronic pain will react to that pain with fear, anger, anxiety, frustration, and other worrisome thoughts and emotions. These thoughts and emotions trigger increased pain by an "amplification" process in the brain.

Thoughts and emotions, whether we are aware of them or whether they are subconscious, are major factors in producing chronic pain and related syndromes. In addition, the stress that frequently accompanies these symptoms, such as decreased activity, decreased income, and more difficult relationships, adds to the problem by making the stress-producing nerve pathways stronger.

In this kind of situation, your brain will continue to produce pain because that's the only way your brain knows how to deal with these stresses. The truth is that your mind can twist your body into a cycle of very real pain.

It is common for people with difficult emotional experiences in their childhood or their recent past to have this same amplification of pain. In fact, certain traumatic experiences in childhood leave an imprint on the brain, making it more likely to develop the vicious pain cycle. People who have a great deal of unresolved stress are also more likely to have chronic pain. Almost everyone has stress to some degree, and in many people it results, sooner or later, in chronic pain that can range from mild and intermittent to intense and unrelenting. And there are many symptoms in addition to pain that can be caused by these wayward connections, such as diarrhea, insomnia, ringing in the ears, fatigue, bladder symptoms, and anxiety. The term I use for this condition is Mind Body Syndrome, or MBS, and most people have some form of it.

What This Program Offers

In the chapters that follow, you will learn about MBS. You will see how it can develop and why modern medicine is typically unable to solve this problem. Most importantly, you'll learn whether you suffer from this syndrome. And finally you'll be guided through a comprehensive program to cure yourself.

As a benefit of this program, you will attain increased self-awareness and greater understanding of how your brain works and of what issues in your life may have contributed to your physical pain. Not only do I expect you to be able to cure your pain, but you will be a stronger, more confident, less anxious, and less vulnerable person.

Your pain is real. But you no longer have to put up with it. This book will show you how to heal yourself. The nerve pathways causing the pain can be retrained by understanding what triggers them and what amplifies them. In order to do this, we must look more closely at the brain and how it is affected by pain and by stress, and how it develops chronic pain pathways. In this way you will finally understand the underlying cause of your pain and begin to take the steps to unlearn your pain.

chapter 2
Medicine's Blind Spot

Too much light often blinds gentlemen of this sort. They cannot see the forest for the trees. — Musarion

I have about come to the conclusion that there is absolutely nothing the matter with me anyway. —Harry S. Truman, on his decision to stop pain medications for neck pain

The key to treating chronic pain and other symptoms is to determine what is causing them. This is not only good medical practice, it is common sense. However, many doctors, whether traditional or holistic, are unaware that learned nerve pathways can produce a large variety of real, physical symptoms. As a result, we have a growing epidemic of pain. Many millions of people suffer, and many billions of dollars are spent on treatments that are often ineffective, such as pain medications, injections, and surgery. Despite the growing amount of money spent on treatment of these painful conditions, the results are disappointing. In fact, a study published in the *Journal of the American Medical Association* found that back and neck pain is increasing in the United States and the cost of caring for such pain has increased to more than $80 billion a year—yet the newest treatments are not any more effective than older treatments, and therefore disability due to back pain is increasing (Martin, et al., 2008).

Over the past five decades, medical science has progressed dramatically in several areas. We have made great strides in understanding and treating cancer, heart disease, stroke, hypertension, diabetes, infectious diseases, and many other illnesses. These achievements have been made possible by a biotechnological approach—by examining these disorders with a very narrow focus to find out what is occurring on a cellular and molecular level. This approach searches for a cure by examining the specific area where the disease is found. We can see the **pathological** changes in the body in people with cancer (a tumor), heart disease (damaged heart tissue), and infections (bacteria causing tissue inflammation). But these types of physically identifiable changes cannot be found in people with Mind Body Syndrome. People with MBS do not have **pathological** changes in their body tissue: they have **physiological** changes that are reversible. That is, they have changes in blood flow, muscle tension, nerve-firing patterns, and brain-wiring patterns that create pain in the *absence* of tissue pathology.

The vast majority of physicians, including me, were trained in the biotechnological approach to medical care. We were taught: "If the back hurts, there must be something wrong with the back." We were not trained to look at the whole person to scrutinize the interaction between a person's social situation and the body, nor to examine how a patients's thoughts and emotions can affect the body.

The advances in understanding pathological processes have led us to believe that we could apply these same biotechnological approaches to chronic painful conditions that have eluded our understanding. This reductionist approach—looking at the problem solely on a tissue or molecular level—does not work when the disorder is Mind Body Syndrome. MBS is caused by a complex set of neurological connections between the brain and the body, rather than a disease localized in one area of the body.

Whiplash

Let's start with a disorder that everyone "knows" is a physical condition: whiplash. Whiplash occurs when someone is in a car accident and the head is thrown backwards, causing strain to the tendons and ligaments of the neck. The neck pain or headaches that result can last for months, years, or even decades. But does this really make sense? If you fracture a bone, you will experience significant pain for a while. But when the fracture begins to heal, the pain will subside. A whiplash injury is a sprain or a strain of the neck, certainly a less serious injury than a fracture. We wouldn't expect an ankle sprain to cause pain for years. So why wouldn't a whiplash injury heal fairly rapidly? The answer lies in the nerve connections. Once these connections are fired due to the injury, they can quickly become learned. They can continue to fire and then become wired so that pain can continue for a long time, even though the ligament strain will typically heal within a week or two.

H. Schrader, a Norwegian neurologist, wondered why there were so many people on disability for whiplash in his country, so he compared the rates of whiplash in Norway to those in Lithuania. In Norway, as in the United States, if you're in a car accident, most doctors recommend rest, heat, and anti-inflammatory medications, hoping to mitigate the effects of the injury. In Lithuania, most doctors advise such patients to simply go back to work. Schrader studied 202 Lithuanians who had been in car accidents and found there were no more people with chronic headaches or neck pain than in a group that had not had car accidents. This was true even for those who had not been wearing seat belts, who had no head rests in their cars, and whose cars were severely damaged (Schrader, et. al., 1996; Schrader, et. al., 2006).

A study by W.H. Castro and colleagues (2001) helps to give us a more complete understanding of whiplash. The researchers put fifty people in a simulation that created the sensation of having the kind of car accident that might cause whiplash. The participants had the experience of an accident, yet their necks did not move at all. Even so, 10 percent of the subjects reported neck pain four weeks after the simulated accident. Why? The researchers found that the people who developed persistent neck pain were the ones who had the most stress and emotional distress in their lives at the time of the experiment. As we shall see, their subconscious minds used the occasion of the experimental "accident" to initiate and perpetuate pain.

Without the mind at work, very few accidents and injuries would cause chronic, lasting pain. A study of demolition derby drivers revealed that almost none had chronic neck pain, even after more than 150 collisions (Simotas and Shen, 2005). Why? Because demolition derby drivers love what they do, and therefore they don't think of the collisions as traumatic. Among most people in Norway and the United States and Canada and many other countries, however, there is an expectation that if you are in a car accident, you may develop whiplash and chronic pain. And, if the accident occurs at a time in your life when there are significant stressors, the chance that chronic pain will develop is greatly increased.

JULIE, A FIFTY-FIVE-YEAR-OLD WOMAN, *had a significant car accident and was shaken up, but the doctors found no broken bones when she was seen in the emergency room. About two days later she developed neck pain, although the rest of her bruises healed and caused her no pain. Her neck, however, got worse and worse. She had X-rays and an MRI that were normal, and therefore she was told it was probably whiplash and that it could last for a long time. She had physical therapy, took painkillers, and rested—all to no avail. Her pain worsened, and she had to wear a neck collar. She stopped going out and became depressed, and the pain got so bad that she cried several times a day. About a year later, she came across Dr. John Sarno's book,* The Mindbody Prescription, *read it, and began to understand that her pain was not caused by the injuries sustained in the accident, but by a set of neurological connections that were triggered by the accident. She realized that she could get better and started doing the exercises recommended in that book. In ten days she was well enough to get rid of her neck collar, and within three weeks she was pain free. She has not had any recurrence of neck pain.*

Back Pain

The situation is very similar for the vast majority of those with back pain and sciatica. There are millions of people with chronic back pain that causes untold suffering, great expense, and huge numbers of medical procedures. Most people think that back and neck pain are degenerative disorders that will inevitably increase with increasing age. However, data from the Center for Disease Control's annual National Health Interview Survey demonstrate that back and neck pain peaks between the ages of forty-five and sixty-four and then actually declines starting at age sixty-five (Strine, 2007).

Doesn't back pain mean that there is a problem in the back? Can't we see the abnormalities of the back on X-rays, CT scans, and MRIs? Actually, no. In three separate studies by M.C. Jensen, D.G. Borenstein, and N. Boos, there was very little correlation between back pain and MRI results (Jensen, et. al., 1994; Borenstein, et. al., 2001; Boos, et. al., 2000). When you take middle-aged people **without any back pain** and give them MRIs, 64 percent of them have bulging discs, degenerative discs, arthritic changes, spinal stenosis, and other common changes. Over time, in some people the MRI results get worse, but the pain decreases; while in others the pain gets worse, though the MRI gets better. Many people with normal MRI findings have severe back pain. In fact, Eugene Carragee of Stanford University wrote in the *New England Journal of Medicine* (2005) that "neither baseline MRIs nor follow-up MRIs are useful predictors of low back pain" and added that "ill-considered attempts to make a diagnosis on the basis of imaging studies may reinforce the suspicion of serious disease, magnify the importance of nonspecific findings, and label patients with spurious diagnoses."

If you have back pain and get an MRI, it is likely your doctor will tell you that the source of your back pain is one of the nonspecific findings Carragee warns about. Studies have shown that only 10 to 15 percent of people with back pain can be accurately diagnosed by available medical tests (Deyo, et. al., 1992). Unfortunately, most physicians (whether they are neurologists, surgeons, or physical medicine specialists) and chiropractors don't heed these studies. When doctors tell a person there is a physical problem in their back based on an MRI result, the patient immediately stops being someone with back pain and starts being someone with a bad back. And if you believe you have a bad back, your pain is more likely to last longer and become more severe.

It is critically important to identify the 10 to 15 percent of back pain sufferers with serious problems by the use of imaging studies. These people typically have a fracture, a tumor, or an infection and need traditional medical treatment or surgery. It is also important to have a physician examine you to make sure there is no evidence of nerve compression or damage, which is demonstrated by a change in reflexes, muscle strength, or loss of sensation. Pain that goes into an arm or leg, tingling, and numb sensations can occur due to MBS, but as long as the examination is normal, this is not evidence of nerve damage.

Back surgery may be necessary for people with clear evidence of nerve damage. But without that evidence, surgery is no better than nonoperative methods for people with sciatic-type and so-called degenerative back pain, according to recent studies in the *Journal of the American Medical Association* and in the *New England Journal of Medicine* (Weinstein, et. al., 2006; Weinstein, et. al., 2007). A recent review of back pain treatment found that neither surgery, injections, or narcotic pain medications have been shown to be effective (Deyo, et. al., 2009). Even more alarming is the finding that back pain outcomes were actually worse in communities with higher rates of surgery (Keller, et. al., 1999). Finally, there is emerging evidence that treatment of chronic pain with narcotic analgesics can actually worsen pain, because narcotics can increase nerve sensitization (Mitra, 2008; Silverman, 2009).

I routinely see people with severe and chronic back pain (including many who were taking morphine or Vicodin or who were on the verge of back surgery) who have had dramatic results in a very short time by using this treatment program for Mind Body Syndrome.

HELEN, A SIXTY-FIVE-YEAR-OLD WOMAN, *had suffered from nine years of back pain. The pain started in her lower back one day while she was working at her job on an automobile assembly line. It was so severe that she had to be carried out of the factory. She was seen by several doctors, and eventually an MRI revealed the following:*

Severe disc space narrowing at L4-L5 and flattened discs at L2-L3 and L3-L4. Disc bulging with flattening of the spinal cord and narrowing of the outlet for the spinal nerves at L2-L3, L3-L4, L4-L5, and L5-S1. The right L4 and L5 nerve roots are compressed by a disc. The facet joints are swollen and there is spinal stenosis.

Helen underwent seven courses of physical therapy, along with massage therapy, acupuncture, electrode nerve stimulation, and specialty care from a pain management clinic. Despite these treatments, her pain continued. It radiated to her right leg and heel, and she began to develop numbness in her left thigh. After nine years on disability leave she finally took an early retirement, and a neurosurgeon scheduled her for lumbar fusion surgery due to the chronic and severe pain. Her physical exam showed normal reflexes, normal muscle strength, and normal sensation despite her symptoms of pain and numbness.

Helen was the oldest of ten siblings. Her father beat her when she was a child, and her mother required her to do a great deal of housework and child care. She recalls going into a closet and screaming, "I hate my parents! I hate my parents!" She had a difficult adult life, which included raising three children by herself, three divorces, and struggles with alcoholism (though Alcoholics Anonymous had helped her remain sober for twenty-seven years). She had many financial difficulties and became very unhappy with her job.

By participating in this program, Helen noted marked pain relief over the first two weeks. The numbness in her thigh disappeared. By the end of the four-week program, she was pain free and canceled her back surgery. Her joy was incalculable, and she felt in control of her body and her life for the first time in nine years.

Four months later, she had a recurrence of back pain one day, but she quickly figured out what caused it. It began on the day she learned that her daughter was scheduled to depart for military duty in Iraq. Recognizing that her emotional stress was responsible for this pain, she used the methods taught in the program to rapidly rid herself of the pain. "In the past, stress would cause pain in my body that would cripple me," Helen said. "But now I look at it, and it goes away."

KATHERINE, A FORTY-TWO-YEAR-OLD WOMAN, *came to me with four years of left buttock and leg pain. Her pain began in the area of her left hamstring while she was running in a ten-kilometer "fun run," an easy task for an active person who had previously run marathons and had regularly hiked, skied, and mountain biked. Despite rest and anti-inflammatory agents, the pain worsened. She then received physical therapy, chiropractic treatments, acupuncture, and massage; she also tried yoga, pilates, and Rolfing, with no improvement.*

MRI scans of her back and X-rays of her hip were normal, and Katherine was diagnosed by different physicians as having a pulled hamstring, ilio-tibial band syndrome, sacroiliac joint instability, and a leg length discrepancy. Despite all of the above therapies, the pain persisted and spread to her hip, outer thigh, and gluteal area. She stopped running and could not do any other physical activities because of the pain. After being seen by a family physician, orthopedic physician, neurologist, and physical medicine specialist with no improvement, Katherine was eventually referred to a nationally renowned medical center. There, she was given a diagnosis of piriformis syndrome and received a steroid injection followed by more physical therapy. Unfortunately, her pain did not diminish, and Katherine continued to spend significant portions of each day in bed or lying on the couch. Over the last few years, she had developed pain in her right scapular area and her right hip as well.

Katherine had experienced tension and migraine headaches as an adolescent. She also suffered from insomnia, fatigue, and depression when she was in her early thirties after her father and mother divorced. Katherine noted multiple stressors over the past several years: she had moved to a new city, her husband had started a new job, her mother had suffered a heart attack, her child had trouble sleeping, and she had renovated her husband's office and her home. She admitted to having high expectations of herself, frequently feeling guilty and being overly conscientious. She told me that she had all but given up on all of her dreams and abilities to live a normal life because of her great pain.

By participating in this program, Katherine was able to connect the occurrence of pain with her life experiences. Her pain diminished within the first two weeks of the program, and she began to resume her normal activities, including running twice a week without pain. After four weeks, she wrote, "I am so happy to say that I now have the ability to recognize that my pain is caused by an accumulation of anger and guilt in my mind and that it uses my body as its outlet and that I no longer allow it to do so. This has taken work on my part; however, I am thankful that I am able to now let go and be pain free."

Fibromyalgia

One of the more enigmatic disorders is fibromyalgia, which means "painful muscles and tissues." People diagnosed with this disorder have chronic widespread pain throughout their bodies, but no one can tell them why. There is no pathological process (no tissue breakdown or destruction) in the bones, joints, tendons, or muscles, yet the pain can be severe and debilitating. Brain imaging studies have shown that the pain is real and is felt as much as pain from a bone fracture (Gracely, et. al., 2002). It is incredibly frustrating for people with widespread pain to have no idea what causes it, to be considered crazy by some, to be considered incurable by others, and to get little or no relief from available pain medications, muscle relaxants, anti-depressants, and mood stabilizers (Wolfe, 2009; Baumgartner, et. al., 2002; Goldenberg, 2004).

People with fibromyalgia also commonly have lower back pain, migraine or tension headaches, temporo-mandibular joint (TMJ) pain, irritable bowel and bladder syndromes, insomnia, or many of the other Mind Body Syndrome symptoms (Geisser, et. al., 2008). Biomedical experts have been able to determine that there is sensitization of pain fibers in the brains of people with fibromyalgia and changes in some of the neurotransmitters in their brains (Yunus, 2007). However, they have not been able to develop any significant breakthrough medical therapies. In fact, very few patients with this condition have been cured or gone into remission through standard medical treatments.

There is ample evidence that people with fibromyalgia have much higher rates of life stressors and victimization (physical, sexual, or emotional abuse) compared to people with other physical disorders and compared to the general population (Goldberg, et. al., 1999; van Houdenhove, et. al., 2001). There is also a large overlap between those with fibromyalgia and those experiencing anxiety, depression, and post-traumatic stress disorder (Cohen, et. al., 2002; Celiker, et. al., 1997). As we shall see in the next chapter, the effects of these stressors are the cause of the painful fibromyalgia symptoms. However, most physicians and researchers can only offer medications to try to cover up the pain. These medications do not lead to cures because they don't get to the root of the problem.

I have seen many people released from the pain of this disorder using the program outlined in this book. If you listen carefully to the full life history of people with fibromyalgia, it becomes crystal clear that it's a form of MBS. In fact, I have conducted research to determine how effective this program is for fibromyalgia, and the results have been gratifying (Hsu, et. al., manuscript submitted). Six weeks after their MBS treatment, approximately 25 percent of patients have gone into remission, meaning their pain has been eliminated or reduced to very low levels. Another 25 percent have experienced a moderate reduction in their pain. These results may not seem remarkable, but consider this: These reductions in pain are long lasting (measured at six months) and exceed the results found in studies of medications. The women with fibromyalgia who were in the control group in this research study were able to use any medications or other treatments. However, none of them showed any evidence of pain reduction. This program requires you to fully understand this model, believe that it applies to you, and be fully committed to the process. People with fibromyalgia and other chronic painful conditions who do these things almost always obtain significant results in this program.

ANJANI, A FORTY-SEVEN-YEAR-OLD WOMAN *who migrated to the United States from India, reached a point in her life when she was beginning to think of doing some more things for herself, such as taking classes at a local college. However, her husband took an extra job, and she had three adolescent children who required a lot of her time. On top of that, her mother-in-law moved into her house and began to lecture her on how to be a better cook, homemaker, and mother. In addition, her brother moved in and expected her to wait on him. Being a dutiful person who put her obligations to others ahead of her own desires, she complied with these additional stressful tasks and cancelled her class, but she had no outlet for her feelings of resentment. Her body reacted to these stresses and suppressed emotions with a widespread painful process, which was labeled as fibromyalgia. After going through this program, her pain was dramatically reduced. One of the keys to her improvement was that she decided to speak up for herself and take more control over her situation at home.*

JANET, A FORTY-ONE-YEAR-OLD WOMAN, *grew up with a mother who was emotionally distant. The mother was very busy with her own life and was usually gone, often playing bridge and tennis. Janet had no illnesses or symptoms of MBS until she was in her thirties.*

She was happily married, with two small children, for whom she was determined to be the best mother possible. She was having a new home built and trying to make it perfect. At this time, she began to develop widespread pain in her muscles and tendons, which was diagnosed as fibromyalgia. When I asked her what her mother was doing at the time she and her children needed her help, she replied, "Playing bridge and tennis." She then began to sob over the loss that she experienced as a child and that her children were now experiencing. Her mother was being as distant with her grandchildren as she had been with her own daughter. At this stressful point in her life, that separation was enough to trigger severe pain in her body. Once she realized that she was not physically ill and that her pain came from unexpressed emotions, her pain totally disappeared.

Headaches and Other Disorders

Tension headaches and migraine headaches afflict millions of people in the United States. More and more people are suffering, and specialized headache clinics have been established for people with severe symptoms. Yet, despite the development of many new medications, we see rising costs of treatment as well as increased loss of productivity due to absences from work and school.

The vast majority of people with chronic headaches have normal CT scans and MRIs. Tests do not detect anything wrong in their brains. As with fibromyalgia, there are many theories about what causes these headaches, from food and chemical sensitivities to genetics. Such things can trigger headaches, but they are not the main underlying cause of these severe and chronic headaches.

Headache specialists do not generally listen very carefully to a patient's life story. Even if they did, they may not be aware that mental events can produce such severe symptoms. When you look very carefully at the onset of headaches and at the precise times they worsen, you will find that conscious and/or subconscious emotions are at the root of the problem.

VICKIE, A FIFTY-FIVE-YEAR-OLD WOMAN, *suffered from constant daily headaches for seventeen years. She had been evaluated by twenty doctors and had been placed on more than twenty different medications in an attempt to control the persistent pain. She had even had a surgical procedure to attempt to relieve pressure on a facial nerve that was thought to be trapped by muscles.*

She had never had headaches until the day when she put on a new pair of prescription glasses and instantly developed pain on the left side of her head that radiated into her face. The pain worsened over the years, and no treatment ever helped.

When I listened carefully to her life story, she told me that her mother was aloof and her father was "bipolar" and unpredictable. Some days, he would come home from work and be fine, but on many occasions he would be in a bad mood and would often grab her by her collar and scream at her. Despite this difficult upbringing, she had no symptoms at all as a child.

At the time when Vickie got the glasses, her home life was fine. However, she had recently gotten a new boss, a woman whom she described as "mean and nasty," who would frequently scream at her.

It became obvious that the new glasses did not cause her headaches, but when she put them on, her subconscious mind used the opportunity to create pain in the same way that a real or simulated car accident can become an opportunity for pain of whiplash. Vickie quit her job a few months later, but by that time the vicious cycle of nerve connections had been formed, and her headaches continued on a daily basis. She started this program, and her headaches gradually began to decrease. After the program, her headaches continued to improve, and after six months she became free of them altogether.

There are several other conditions that are typically manifestations of MBS, such as chronic abdominal pain and pelvic pain, TMJ pain, irritable bowel syndrome, irritable bladder syndrome (known as interstitial cystitis), chronic fatigue, tinnitus, and insomnia. See the table at the end of this chapter for a list of common syndromes caused by MBS. If a careful medical evaluation does not show any clear pathologic process, then the symptoms in these conditions are likely caused by a vicious cycle of nerve connections that have been learned by the mind and body.

Standard Treatment Equals Faulty Diagnosis

What happens if you develop any of these MBS symptoms and seek care from your physician? The doctor will rarely take a careful enough history to determine if the symptoms may be related to stressful events and emotions. However, your doctor will usually do thorough medical testing to look for serious disorders such as cancer, immune disorders, fractures, and heart and vascular diseases. These tests are very important to make sure you don't have a tissue breakdown disease. If the tests find no clear evidence of disease, you may become more anxious because there is no clear explanation for the symptoms, and the doctor may be puzzled and imply that the pain is all in your head. This is one of the worst things a doctor can say to someone. Mind Body Syndrome is a real condition, and it can be effectively treated. It is not imaginary or brought on because the patient wants to be sick. Many people that I see are frustrated with their doctors for not explaining what is going on and why they are in pain. The reason most doctors don't adequately explain chronic pain is that they don't understand this disorder.

If the doctor finds something on an MRI such as a degenerating disc or bulging disc or spinal stenosis, the patient will often be led to believe there is a serious medical condition. Once someone is told that they have fibromyalgia, they may be initially relieved to discover that there is a name for their severe symptoms. However, once they are told that they will have to manage the pain since there are no effective treatments to cure it, they are likely to become upset and depressed.

Traditional medical treatments are geared towards correcting the underlying pathology in the body. In MBS, there are reversible physiological changes to the brain and nerve pathways, but there is no underlying tissue breakdown. Standard treatments don't address the true cause of these symptoms but try to cover them up. Pain medications, migraine medications, stomach and bladder medications, physical therapy, acupuncture, vitamins, herbs, and all of the other therapies recommended for these disorders will often provide at most a partial or a temporary relief. When these therapies and medications do work for people with MBS, it is usually due to the placebo effect, that is, the expectation by the patient that the treatment will work (Bausell, 2007; Brody and Brody, 2001). With this belief, the mind allows the treatment to work—but often the relief is only temporary, since the person has not understood what caused the problem in the first place.

Despite the absence of confirmed pathology, the doctor will often make a diagnosis. Medicine has given names to these clusters of symptoms: fibromyalgia, migraine headaches, sciatica, interstitial cystitis, TMJ disorder. This labeling is often harmful. The patient now thinks he or she has a serious condition, and websites for these conditions support the belief that the condition could be severe and long lasting.

The medical profession has unwittingly created a form of mental imprisonment that I call medicalization, when diagnosis and treatment causes an increase in pain and suffering. The false belief that one has a serious and intractable condition causes activation of more stress and emotional reactions, such as depression, hopelessness, helplessness, fear, and anxiety, that can exacerbate the problem. In addition, the costs associated with such faulty diagnoses are staggering. It is estimated that up to one third of the medical care in the U.S. is unnecessary (Brownlee, 2007).

The first critical step in dealing with chronic symptoms is to get the correct diagnosis. If there is a tissue breakdown disorder, then I would recommend traditional medical treatments. If you have been suffering for some time, if your doctors haven't been able to adequately explain why you have so much pain, if your only options are injections or pain medications, then you are likely to have MBS. If the true diagnosis is Mind Body Syndrome, then traditional medical therapies are not likely to cure the condition. Your doctors have not been able to help you because they have been looking in the wrong place.

Conditions that are Commonly Caused By Mind Body Syndrome

CHRONIC PAIN SYNDROMES

Tension headaches
Migraine headaches
Back pain
Neck pain
Whiplash
Fibromyalgia
Temporomandibular joint
   (TMJ) syndrome
Chronic abdominal and
   pelvic pain syndromes
Chronic tendonitis
Vulvodynia
Piriformis syndrome
Sciatic pain syndrome
Repetitive stress injury
Foot pain syndromes
Myofascial pain syndrome

AUTONOMIC NERVOUS SYSTEM RELATED DISORDERS

Irritable bowel syndrome
Interstitial cystitis (Irritable
   bladder syndrome)
Postural orthostatic
   tachycardia syndrome
Inappropriate sinus
   tachycardia
Reflex sympathetic dystrophy
   (Chronic regional pain
   disorder)
Functional dyspepsia

OTHER SYNDROMES

Insomnia
Chronic fatigue syndrome
Paresthesias (numbness,
   tingling, burning)
Tinnitus
Dizziness
Spasmodic dysphonia
Chronic hives
Anxiety
Depression
Obsessive-compulsive
   disorder
Post-traumatic stress disorder

NOTE: *Many of the symptoms in this table can be caused by physical disorders that require medical treatment. Consult your doctor or a specialist in Mind Body Medicine (see the Appendix) to determine if you can participate in this program. See Chapter 5 for help in determining if you have Mind Body Syndrome.*

chapter 3
How Pain Develops: The Role of the Brain

Human beings owe a surprisingly large proportion of their cognitive
and behavioral capacities to the existence of an "automatic self"
of which they have no conscious knowledge and over which they
have little voluntary control. — Jonathan Miller

Why do so many people have pain and other symptoms caused by Mind Body Syndrome? How do the brain and the body learn the vicious cycle of pain? The key to understanding the answers is to recognize how stress and emotions play a vital role in the initiation and perpetuation of pain.

We live in a stressful world to which we have not fully adapted. Our brains are wired to react to the very different, ancient world of our ancestors. They experienced acute stress—for example, dangerous animals—on an occasional basis. The brain often has trouble dealing with the chronic stresses of today. That's why, when stress becomes chronic and we feel trapped in situations for which there is no easy way out, we can easily develop a set of nerve connections that are painful.

You already know that stress causes physical reactions. Your face will turn red if you are embarrassed. That's because your emotions cause the autonomic nervous system to increase blood flow to the face. This is a very real bodily response to an emotion. If you have a stressful day at work or at school, you might get a headache; this is also real pain caused by emotions. If you have to give a speech in front of hundreds of people, your stomach may tighten up from nervousness. These are normal everyday reactions caused by the connections between the brain and the body. Everyone accepts that these are physical reactions to stressful events, that they are not signs of disease, and that the symptoms will disappear when the stress that triggers them subsides.

This is exactly the mechanism of Mind Body Syndrome: Stress triggers emotions that cause our bodies to react by producing physical symptoms. The symptoms are real. Your face really does turn red when you blush from embarrassment. Your head or your stomach really does hurt if you've had a difficult day or face a daunting challenge. The symptoms, including the pain, are not imaginary. They are physical processes. They are real. But they are physiological processes that can be reversed. They are temporary.

If you have these symptoms, you're not crazy. You're normal. Almost everyone has some physical symptoms due to the body's reaction to stress. I have asked hundreds of people during my lectures if they know where they "hold" stress in their bodies, and almost everyone has an answer. It is common knowledge that stress can cause physical reactions.

What is not common knowledge is that stress and emotions can create the nerve pathways that can cause chronic and often severe physical symptoms. The cure for such chronic pain or other symptoms is not a drug or a remedy designed to lessen or cover up these symptoms. If you do not find and treat the underlying cause of the pain, you will not get better. For most people, the underlying cause is that the emotional reactions to stress trigger nerve connections that create physical pain. Instead of addressing our emotional conflicts that are at the bottom of our distress, many of us have developed ways to medicate ourselves. But medicating with alcohol, drugs, work, or other means does not resolve anything, and can just create further problems, including addiction, further stress, and social isolation.

The Emotional Brain

The way our brains work explains how the stresses of life can turn into bodily pain. Though our brains are very complicated and everyone reacts differently to different stresses, we share some things in common. We all need to be loved, nurtured, and protected. We all need to grow, develop, and become independent. We all have thoughts and emotions and memories.

Our emotional memories are imprinted in our brains and stored in what are called associative networks (LeDoux, 1996). They are imprinted in a part of the brain called the amygdala, the center where emotions are registered and stored. The amygdala is closely connected to the hypothalamus, the center for the autonomic nervous system (ANS) (van der Kolk, 1994; Okifuji and Turk, 2002). The ANS controls our breathing, heart rate, blood pressure, temperature, and many other automatic and involuntary functions—the things our body does without our conscious mind being aware of them.

During times of stress, the amygdala sends signals to activate the ANS and produce the hormones cortisol and adrenaline, which turn on the "fight or flight" reaction. That's a system that directs blood flow to muscles to get our body ready to run or do battle, and it causes our bodies to react instantly before we are aware of what is going on. Human beings developed this system during the evolutionary process to help our chances for survival.

If we see something squiggly moving across the ground, our autonomic nervous system causes us to immediately jump back to protect ourselves. We do not stop and reach out to see what the squiggly thing is. That conscious action could get us killed. Our protective system kicks in before we have the chance to think. In fact, research shows that when emotions arise quickly, the blood flow in the brain shifts away from the frontal lobes, the conscious thinking part of the brain, to the limbic system, which is the emotional, reacting, and subconscious part of the brain, which includes the amygdala and the autonomic nervous system (Takamatsu, et. al., 2003).

The Role of the Autonomic Nervous System

The autonomic nervous system controls the nerve fibers that affect every area of your body. Studies have shown that emotions such as anxiety or anger cause increased tension in the back muscles of people with chronic back pain (Burns, et. al., 2006; Quartana and Burns, 2007). This muscle tension, which typically takes place without our conscious awareness, can cause real and severe physical pain. Often we are not even aware of the emotions that are triggering these automatic physical responses, which is why they are referred to as subconscious or unconscious emotions.

There is a large variety of processes that can occur with ANS activation. Not only are muscles and blood flow involved, but the nervous system, the heart, the gastrointestinal (GI) system, and the genito-urinary (GU) systems can all be altered. And the ANS can produce very specific changes, depending on the specific situation, that will vary from person to person and from moment to moment (Levenson, 1992; Burns, et. al., 2006). A careful understanding of the reactions of animals to stressful situations reveals that they may fight or flee, but they may also freeze (as a rabbit will do) or submit (play dead) (LeDoux, 1996). The ANS can produce a much greater variety of symptoms in response to stress and emotional reactions in humans. Activation of the muscles can produce pain in almost any part of the body. Nervous system activation can produce tingling, numbness, or burning sensations as well as dizziness, tinnitus, and anxiety. GI and GU system activation can produce irritable bowel and bladder syndromes. Cardiovascular (CV) activation can produce palpitations and a rapid heart rate. Alterations in blood flow can produce migraine headaches. And the freeze and submission responses typically cause fatigue and/or depression.

Pain caused by ANS activation can occur suddenly with an acute spasm of muscles, or it can develop gradually over time. It can occur in the back, neck, head, abdomen, pelvis, or almost anywhere in the body. This pain can be constant or occasional, it can be mild or severe, and it can feel like an ache, a numbness, or a shooting pain. For people who suffer in these various ways in various places because of Mind Body Syndrome, there is no tissue breakdown or physical disease in the body. Yet, the pain is real.

Pain in the Brain

In addition to the amygdala and the ANS, there are other areas in the brain that affect whether and how we feel pain. One part of the brain that mediates pain is known as the anterior cingulate cortex (ACC). Emotional responses increase the activity of this area, causing pain to become amplified. When you feel pain, this may cause worry about what it is; when you go to the doctor and you're told you have a problem in your back or neck, this may cause fear; when your doctor tells you that he or she doesn't know what is causing the pain, this may cause resentment; when the pain becomes chronic and you don't know if you'll ever get better, this may cause frustration. All of these emotional reactions activate the ACC. MRI studies show that when the ACC is activated, pain is greatly increased (Klossika, et. al., 2006; Peyron, et. al., 2000). In addition, when the ACC is activated, it turns off the dorsolateral prefrontal cortex (DLPFC) area of the brain, a part of the brain that acts to decrease pain (Lieberman, et. al., 2004).

In addition, chronic stress produces increased sensitivity to pain in the brain, the spinal cord, and the nerves. Certain cytokines (proteins that send messages to other parts of the body) are released during times of stress, and these cytokines cause cells and nerve endings to be more sensitive to pain (Aubert, 2008; Alesci, et. al., 2005).

The Role of Stress in Childhood

It is not only current stress that can trigger painful reactions. Emotional experiences in childhood are imprinted in the amygdala. Several studies show that animals exposed in infancy to very stressful environments (such as separation from their mother or being exposed to painful stimuli) grow up to have overly active autonomic nervous system responses (McEwen, 1998; Arborelius and Eklund, 2007). Human infants who are exposed to repeated blood drawing within the first few weeks of life have increased pain when they have medical procedures several months later (Taddio and Katz, 2005). Adults who are exposed to traumatic events in childhood such as emotional, physical, or sexual abuse have a much greater chance of developing chronic pain (as well as anxiety and other psychological disturbances) (Anda, et. al., 2006). The emotional imprinting from early experiences is stored in the amygdala, and when a similar experience occurs later in life, the ANS reaction can start a painful process.

Researchers can measure markers of chronic stress, such as abnormalities in an ANS hormone, cortisol. One study found that adults who have abnormalities in cortisol production are more likely to develop chronic pain than those who do not have these abnormalities (McBeth, et. al., 2007). This further cements the powerful relationship between chronic stress and chronic pain.

How an Injury Can Start a Cycle of Pain

Sometimes the pain cycle is started by an injury, such as a strain, a sprain, or a fracture. When the injury occurs, the pain signals in the body and brain get fired. Usually these signals will decrease, and the pain will go away when the injury heals. Most acute injuries will heal within a few weeks. That is how long it usually takes for the body to repair any tissue breakdown that has occurred. After that, if the pain does not go away, there is something else going on. Many people are suffering from chronic pain that they believe is caused by an injury that occurred several months or years ago. That doesn't make sense, because fractures of even our biggest bones will heal in several weeks. The injury itself—whether from a sprain or a strain such as a whiplash injury—is not causing the pain. But an injury can trigger a series of events that lead to chronic pain.

That's especially true if there are stressful life circumstances occurring around the same time as the injury. If so, it is much more likely that the pain signals set in motion by the injury will become learned, and a vicious cycle of pain will develop. It is well known among neuroscientists that when the nerves that carry pain signals from the site of an injury to the brain are activated for some time, the nerves become "sensitized," meaning they are more likely to fire and send more pain signals with lesser amounts of tissue activation (Staud and Smitherman, 2002; Giesecke, et. al., 2004). This is how, over time, acute pain can become chronic, although the tissues have healed from the acute injury. The small nerves learn to react to even very minor changes, such as tense muscles, which are easily triggered by an overly active ACC and ANS. This process of sensitization has been shown to occur in people with fibromyalgia and chronic back pain (Giesecke, 2004).

These sensitized nerves that carry pain signals to the brain gradually affect the brain as well. The areas of painful sensation in the brain also become sensitized and continue to experience pain. This is another way that chronic pain caused by Mind Body Syndrome becomes engrained. As the neurological system of the brain and body learns these pain and other symptom pathways, these nerve fibers very quickly start to get wired together. The more often nerves fire, the longer the pain occurs, and the more likely these fibers will continue to create this vicious cycle of pain. Scientists use the terms brain reorganization and neuroplasticity to describe the brain's ability to create new pathways. It has been shown that acute pain can induce changes in the spinal cord and brain, which can lead to increased pain (Baranauskas, 2001) and can enlarge over time, creating chronic pain (Melzack, et. al.,1999).

The fact that pain can be felt in an area that is not diseased has been illustrated in phantom limb syndrome, where an amputee experiences pain that feels like it is coming from the part of the body that's been amputated. Phantom limb syndrome is a perfect example of Mind Body Syndrome— pain is felt in an area that is clearly not diseased. The pain is caused by nerve sensitization and brain reorganization producing pain, which is felt in the missing limb (Flor, et. al., 1995).

Going one step further, a group of researchers tried to determine if the brain could actually create pain (Derbyshire, et. al., 2004). They took a group of people and exposed them to three distinct conditions; thermal pain in one hand, the hypnotic suggestion that they were feeling thermal hand pain, and simply imagining feeling thermal hand pain while not under hypnosis. Their brains were imaged to see if there were differences between these three conditions. The brain images showed that similar areas were activated in the thermal pain and the hypnotic pain situations (including the ACC and a few other areas), while fewer and different brain areas were activated during imagined pain. This was the first evidence that the brain can create pain that is indistinguishable from pain caused by stimulation of nerves in tissues. This research helps confirm that real pain can be caused by either physical disease states or by processes that primarily involve the brain, as with Mind Body Syndrome.

Thoughts and Pain

A great deal of research over the past twenty years has also demonstrated how important the brain is in modulating pain. All pain has sensory, cognitive, and affective components (Wager, et. al., 2004). The **sensory** component includes descriptions of how pain is felt, such as aching, burning, sharpness, or numbing. The **cognitive** component is what you think about the pain: what the cause is, whether you believe it is temporary or permanent, controllable, or curable. The **affective** component consists of your feelings and emotions about the pain, such as fear, worry, anger, and resentment. There are distinct areas of the nervous system that process these three components of pain (Melzack and Casey, 1968; Ploner et. al., 1999; Vogt and Sikes, 2000; Ochsner et. al., 2008). In order to eliminate chronic pain, all of the components need to be addressed. The ways in which people think about their pain and the feelings that are connected to it have great impact on the severity of the pain.

M.D. Lieberman and colleagues (2004) conducted a study in which people with irritable bowel syndrome were treated with a placebo pill. In those who responded with fewer symptoms (less pain, diarrhea, or constipation), they found that the anterior cingulate cortex was inactivated in the brain while the dorsolateral prefrontal cortex (DLPFC) was activated. Those whose symptoms did not decrease had the opposite brain response: an activated ACC and inactivated DLPFC. This study demonstrates that what we think about our condition—the cognitive components of our pain—affects how our brain controls pain and other Mind Body Syndrome symptoms.

In a study published in the *Journal of the American Medical Association* (Waber, et. al., 2008), a group of researchers tested the pain responses of volunteers to a bracelet that gave gradated levels of electric shocks. All participants were first given a pill that they were told was a new medication similar to codeine, but faster acting. Half of the subjects were told that it cost about $2.50 per pill, while the others were told that each pill cost ten cents. Though all the pills were placebos, those who received the more "expensive" pills felt significantly less pain from the bracelet shocks than did those who were given the supposedly cheaper pills.

In a research study of people with chronic hand pain due to an ANS dysfunction condition known as chronic regional pain syndrome (or reflex sympathetic dystrophy), subjects were shown pictures of hands in different positions. They were asked to imagine moving their hand into those positions. Results showed that they had increased pain and swelling of their hands just from imagining moving them (Moseley, et. al., 2008).

These studies demonstrate that what we think about pain can have a great impact on how we actually feel pain. Many studies also show how emotions affect how we experience pain.

Emotions and Pain

Several studies demonstrate the connection between emotions and chronic pain. There is a large overlap between Mind Body Syndrome and different types of anxiety disorders. More than a third of people with fibromyalgia or irritable bowel syndrome have high rates of post-traumatic stress disorder (PTSD) (Amir, et. al., 1997; Sherman, et. al., 2000). One study of a group of military veterans with PTSD showed 80 percent of them had chronic pain (Beckham, 1997). In a study of people with obsessive-compulsive disorder (OCD), situations that triggered their OCD symptoms were associated with an activated ACC in the brain (Fitzgerald, et. al., 2005).

John Burns (2006) studied pain thresholds in people with chronic low back pain. He found that when they recalled a time that had made them angry, they had increased activation of the lower back muscles and experienced more pain. They did not show increases in heart rate or blood pressure and did not have activation of muscle groups unrelated to the areas of pain, which shows that their bodies reacted to anger in a very specific area. In another study, volunteers were put in a situation that created either anxiety or anger and then instructed to either express their feelings normally, try to inhibit their feelings, or try not to show any feelings. After this they placed one hand in ice water. Those who were instructed not to feel or show anxiety or anger had less tolerance for the pain (Quartana and Burns, 2007). Finally, patients with low back pain were instructed to either suppress or not suppress anger during a stressful laboratory experiment. Those instructed to suppress their emotions reported more pain, both during and after the experiment (Burns, et. al., 2008). Together these studies show that both anxiety and anger can cause a lower pain threshold and can increase muscle tension. Suppression of emotions leads to even higher pain levels.

Brain imaging studies have also revealed the strong relationship between emotions and pain. For example, Eisenberger and her colleagues (2003 and 2006) have shown that when people are put in a laboratory situation where they are excluded or rejected by others, the ACC is activated and pain sensitivity is enhanced. The ACC is also activated by fear and worry, as is the amygdala and the ANS (Fitzgerald, et. al., 2005; Das, et. al., 2005). When pain develops, if we are unsure why it's there and our doctors are unable to explain it or make it go away, most people begin to worry about the pain and to fear that it will become a constant problem. These emotions then trigger pain pathways in the brain to become more pronounced, which, of course, tends to exacerbate the pain (Bailey, et. al., 2009; Asmundson and Katz, 2009). A vicious cycle of pain, fear of pain, decreased activity, and worry often ensues. When this happens, chronic pain becomes a way of life, and there is no way out of it until the thoughts and feelings which are driving the pain are addressed. For an excellent description of this phenomenon as seen in chronic back pain, see *Back Sense* (Siegel, et. al., 2005).

A unique study was conducted with a group of healthy volunteers and a group of people who had recovered from significant depression (Hooley, et. al., 2005). Both groups had brain MRIs taken while they listened to a tape recording of their own mothers, who had recorded thirty seconds of praise and also thirty seconds of criticism. Both groups had increases in their DLPFC activation when listening to the praise. When the healthy volunteers listened to the criticism, they also had increases in the DLPFC (demonstrating their resiliency to stress), but those with a history of depression had decreases in DLPFC activation, putting them at risk for developing pain. To summarize, when we experience difficult or stressful situations, especially if we have had significant stresses earlier in life and if we are unable to express or show how we feel, we will be at risk for our bodies to experience pain.

The Triggers of Pain

Once a pain cycle is initiated between the brain and the body, certain "triggers" will usually begin to develop and add to the painful responses. Most people have heard of the experiments of Ivan Pavlov, the Russian scientist, who rang a buzzer when he fed his dogs (Cunningham, 2001). He soon noticed the dogs would salivate when the buzzer rang, even if there was no food in sight. Their brains had learned that a buzzer meant food, so their bodies reacted accordingly. Several years ago, Robert Ader gave some mice cyclophosphamide, a powerful immune-suppressing medication, in a bowl with saccharine, which has a peculiar taste. Predictably, their immune systems became significantly suppressed. A few weeks later, after their immune systems recovered, he gave them a bowl with just saccharine. Their immune systems again became suppressed, demonstrating the power of triggers (Cohen, et. al., 1979). This study has been replicated in people as well (Goebel, et. al., 2002).

It is easy to see how certain triggers can develop in people with Mind Body Syndrome. Once a pain pathway (say, a headache) has started, if it occurs during a stressful situation that also happens to coincide with eating a certain food, or drinking red wine, or seeing a certain kind of light, or meeting a certain person, the brain will learn that association. Then the next time you are exposed to that chemical or situation, the headache can recur. This is called conditioning. Physical activities can also be triggers. For example, someone with back pain will notice that walking, driving, sitting, or bending over will cause pain, and these actions will be associated with pain and become triggers for the pain. Over time, the pathways connecting these triggers to the pain will become stronger, and the pain cycle will become very well learned by the brain and the body.

Fortunately, these triggers can be overcome or, in psychological terms, extinguished, by unlearning this connection. The program in this book will teach you how to break these triggers that perpetuate pain and other Mind Body Syndrome symptoms.

Priming of Pain

Another important concept to understand is that of "priming." When we learn how to ride a bicycle or throw a ball, those nerve pathways become engrained. Even if we haven't been on a bike or thrown a ball in several years, when we need to, those pathways will be activated, and we will perform that skill. Nerve impulses that are caused by a physical injury, such as a car accident or a fall, create a pain pathway between the brain and the body, which will typically diminish over a few days or weeks as the damaged body tissues heal. However, the pain pathways can lie dormant, and at some time in the future, if situations occur that create significant stress and emotional reactions, these pain pathways can re-emerge to create the same type of pain.

I evaluated a young woman with severe back pain. As a teenager, she had sustained a mild back injury from a fall during an athletic competition. Her injury healed, and she was fine for several years. However, when her fiancé broke off their engagement just prior to the wedding date, she developed back pain in the same area, although no new injury occurred. Her brain was primed to have back pain in that specific area, and it created pain in a place that was convenient since it had already been learned.

The diagram on the next page shows how the brain and body can learn to produce chronic pain or other symptoms.

Neurologic Mechanism for Mind Body Syndrome

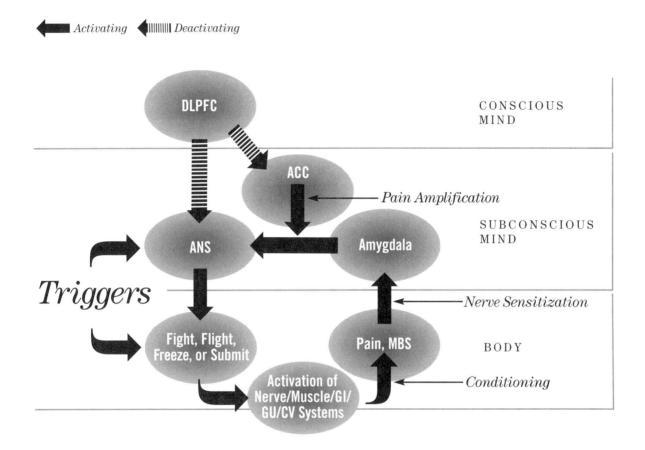

THE PATHWAYS THAT PRODUCE AND PERPETUATE MIND BODY SYNDROME: These pathways can begin due to an injury or stressful event that produces strong emotions in the amygdala. Once the pain begins, nerves that send pain signals to the brain become sensitive over time and send repeated signals even when there is no tissue damage in the area where the pain is felt. These signals go to the amygdala and then get amplified by both conscious and subconscious emotions, which trigger activation of the anterior cingulate cortex (ACC). The autonomic nervous system (ANS) activates the fight, flight, freeze, or submit mechanism, which produces nerve activation, muscle tension, GI/GU spasm, and/or CV activation that worsens the physical symptoms. These pathways get reinforced over time, and this creates a vicious cycle of pain and increased emotional responses. A variety of triggers (such as certain physical movements or positions, places, weather changes, foods, or situations) can act as conditioned responses and add to the neurologic pathways that perpetuate pain. In the conscious portion of the brain, the dorsolateral prefrontal cortex (DLPFC) area can act to diminish and break the cycle by overriding the activity of the ANS and by deactivating the ACC.

How the Brain Stops Pain

Fortunately, the dorsolateral prefrontal cortex, which is in the conscious part of the brain (the frontal lobe), can reverse the vicious cycle of pain by controlling the subconscious pathways that produce Mind Body Syndrome. The DLPFC is so powerful that it can eliminate painful experiences. It has been shown that people who habitually cut themselves with razor blades have much more tolerance for physical pain. When their brains are scanned, their DLPFC area is very active, demonstrating the power that this brain area can have over pain (Schmahl, et. al., 2006).

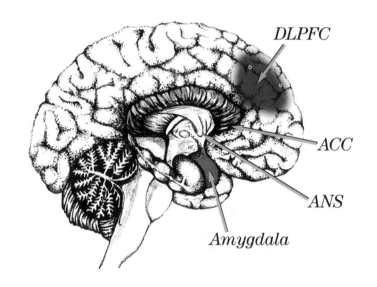

When the DLPFC is activated, the ACC—the area that exacerbates pain—is automatically deactivated, thus further reducing pain. Schmahl and colleagues (2006) have shown that people can learn to decrease the ACC and increase the DLPFC and therefore reduce pain as well as psychological symptoms. The exercises in this book are designed to increase activation of the DLPFC, decrease activation in the ACC and the ANS, extinguish triggers that perpetuate pain, and diminish the emotional responses from the amygdala. The reason that this program is so effective in curing Mind Body Syndrome is that the program corrects the underlying causes of the pain, therefore breaking the cycle of pain.

The processes of an overactive ANS and ACC which produce excessive muscle tension and spasm—and become triggered by a variety of activities, chemicals, and situations—are the cause of the majority of neck aches, back pains, tension headaches, migraines, intestinal spasms and discomfort, bladder spasms, the overall body pains of fibromyalgia, and many other conditions that are forms of Mind Body Syndrome. If you have these conditions, and standard tests have not identified any clear medical pathology, then you can be reassured that there is none. That is really good news. If your condition is caused by Mind Body Syndrome, rather than a pathologic disease in the body, then a cure is truly possible. All you have to do is figure out what physical and psychological processes have helped to create and perpetuate the symptoms and then work on activating the DLPFC in order to extinguish the neurological vicious cycle. That is what this program does: it helps you rewire your brain and unlearn your pain.

chapter 4

How Pain Develops: The Role of the Mind

We must never take a person's testimony, however sincere, that he has felt nothing, as proof positive that no feeling has been there. — William James

The Psychological Basis for Mind Body Syndrome

Many people have trouble accepting that severe pain and other dramatic symptoms can be caused wholly by the interaction between the mind and the body. Not only is it true, it is common. Bodily reactions to mental events occur in most people on a regular basis—we just don't notice them, or we attribute them to purely physical causes. The truth is that the body is a barometer of the mind, and it reflects what is going on in the mind every minute of every day. Once you are aware of this connection, you will see the signs in yourself and your family and friends on a regular basis.

After I gave a lecture a few years ago, a physician approached me and told me his story. He was wounded in the Vietnam war and came home with shrapnel in one leg, after his unit came under attack and several of his buddies were also injured or killed. He regained full function of his leg, became a doctor, worked at a great job, and had a wonderful family. Occasionally, "out of the blue," he would start to limp and have leg pain that would last for a few minutes and then go away. He had no idea why, but it recurred every year or two. One day, a few years ago, during an episode of leg pain and limping, his wife said to him, "Do you hear that helicopter?" He replied, "No, I didn't, but I hear it now." And the next time he began limping, there was a helicopter overhead. As soon as he recognized that the sound of a helicopter triggered his limping, the limping vanished. At a subconscious level in his brain, the sound reminded him of his traumatic experiences during the war and caused his body to react, without him even being aware of the sound that had triggered his physical reaction.

A Brief History of Mind Body Syndrome

To help understand how MBS develops, let's first look at the history of how psychological mechanisms have caused disorders now recognizable as MBS. In the 1600s through the 1800s, a common response to significant stress was paralysis in a limb. This sudden inability to use an arm or leg was not due to tissue disease, stroke, or damage to the nervous system. In those days, this type of paralysis was viewed as a common medical condition, rather than as a physical manifestation of psychological distress. In modern times, we call this a conversion disorder because there is no pathology in the brain or body—yet the affected person cannot move the "paralyzed" arm or leg.

In the 1930s, a physician reported on the case of a young nun who left the convent and secretly married without her parents' knowledge. As she sat down to write her parents a letter about what she had done, she could not move her arm. Later that day, she went to church for confession and suddenly was unable to speak. This was clearly a case of significant symptoms being caused by the subconscious mind. Though she may not have felt extremely distressed, her subconscious mind acted to prevent her from revealing the marriage either verbally or in writing—probably because of significant fear and/or guilt (Harriman, 1935).

An important advance in medicine was the discovery of deep tendon reflexes. The simple test of striking a tendon with a reflex hammer can quickly distinguish pathological from psychological paralysis. Amazingly, once doctors could do this test, the number of people with this type of conversion disorder decreased substantially, and now the condition is rare. When doctors and the general public come to view a medical condition as psychologically induced, it is less likely to occur. See *From Paralysis to Fatigue* for an excellent discussion of this phenomena (Shorter, 1992).

Choices of the Mind

The subconscious mind is unlikely to produce symptoms that will be easily seen as psychological. But since humans continue to experience great stresses and strong emotions, paralysis has been replaced by chronic back pain, fibromyalgia, fatigue, irritable bowel syndrome, and many other symptoms (Shorter, 1992).

Most medical students have seen that some of their classmates will tend to get certain symptoms when they learn about them in school. This type of suggestibility is a form of what's known as social contagion. Nicholas Christakis and James Fowler have studied social contagion and found that smoking, obesity, and happiness are all at least partially determined by contact with people whom we see socially or at work (Christakis and Fowler, 2008; Christakis and Fowler, 2007; Fowler and Christakis, 2008). In Germany, surveys of the prevalence of back pain were done for several years in both East and West Germany, beginning with the fall of the Berlin Wall and the reunification of Germany (Raspe, et. al., 2008). The levels of back pain were much lower in East Germany prior to reunification, but these levels rose to meet the levels of back pain in West Germany after the two countries merged. The authors gave this reason: "We hypothesize that back pain is a communicable disease and suggest a harmful influence of back-related beliefs and attitudes transmitted from West to East Germany via mass media and personal contacts." We are bombarded with television ads for medications for restless leg syndrome, fibromyalgia, migraine headaches, and insomnia—all of which are typically forms of MBS. These ads actually increase the number of people who get these conditions, because the subconscious mind will be more likely to create and perpetuate these common symptoms when stressful situations occur in life.

The symptoms that occur when we are under significant stress can vary greatly. I saw a teenager who developed a variety of symptoms over the course of a year. I was certain these symptoms were all caused by MBS, because extensive medical testing showed no tissue breakdown disorders and he recovered fully with MBS treatment. He was going through a significant amount of family stress and developed hip pain, then headaches, then chest pain, then fainting spells, then stomach pains, then the headaches again, then leg pains. All these symptoms were caused by the subconscious mind creating physical symptoms in response to his stressful situation. Interestingly, he never developed any signs of anxiety or depression, which are common in adults with MBS. This would have been less acceptable to him as a young male, so his mind "chose" other pathways to express the tension.

A few years ago, I saw a young man who had developed severe pain. His sister had died suddenly, and during the mourning period he was invited to a bachelor's party for a friend. He didn't think he should attend, but his friends convinced him to go. At the party, there was a lot of drinking and nudity, and he received an erotic massage. The next morning he woke up with pain in his groin. He went to many different doctors—including urologists, neurologists, pain doctors, and anesthesiologists—and even a nationally renowned medical center. Each doctor heard the same story, "I just woke up with this pain one day," and none asked about the context of his life. He was treated with many different medications, painkillers, injections, and nerve blocks—to no avail. But it's pretty obvious that the cause for his pain was his conflicted feelings about going to the party. The groin pain was a manifestation of guilt. This is a good example of the theory that strong emotions are often too dangerous or disturbing to be felt or expressed and therefore these emotions are kept in the subconscious by means of suppression. The resultant tension in the mind is expressed as pain or other MBS symptoms as a distraction or a warning from these strong subconscious emotions (Sarno, 2006). After three painful years, the young man finally sought treatment for Mind Body Syndrome and became pain free.

The Subconscious Mind

Many studies document the role of the subconscious mind in determining human behavior. It is estimated that approximately 95 percent of our thoughts, feelings, and memories reside in the subconscious (Wilson, 2002). While a human brain can take in about eleven million bits of information each second, the conscious brain can process only about forty bits. We are responding each moment to a huge amount of information being poured into our subconscious minds (Wilson, 2002).

Most of our daily actions are guided by our subconscious mind. We learn how to do routine things, and these actions become automatic—how we chew and swallow, how we walk, speak, drive a car, throw a baseball. We don't consciously think about how to do these things, we just do them. As described in *Strangers to Ourselves: Discovering the Adaptive Unconscious* by Timothy Wilson (2002) and by Daniel Wegner in *The Illusion of Conscious Will* (2002), these routine actions are all produced by learned neurological patterns in the subconscious part of the brain.

What about thoughts and actions that are not so commonly performed? What about things that we decide to do, such as which clothes to wear, what to order at a restaurant, whom to ask for a date? These acts too are controlled to a great degree by the subconscious mind. As described by Wegner, we are not consciously aware of most actions until we perform them. Even the simplest act of lifting a finger has been shown to have a subconscious component that occurs in the brain before we are aware that we have decided to lift the finger (Wegner, 2002).

Many research studies show that our subconscious mind drives our reactions to everyday situations. In one study, people subliminally presented with words such as "old," "wise," "retired," and "gray" walked more slowly from the room than a control group who were presented with random words (Bargh, 1996). People who were shown aggressive words in a subliminal fashion interpreted behavior of others as being more hostile (Bargh and Pietromonaco, 1982), and those who were shown subliminal words related to assertiveness were more likely to interrupt the investigator than those who were shown subliminal words related to politeness (Bargh, 1990). People who briefly held an iced coffee drink in their hand rated a stranger as being less friendly than did people who held a warm cup of coffee (Williams, 2008).

Reactions to Stress

As we grow up, we are exposed to certain stressful events, and the emotional memories associated with these events are stored in the amygdala. When physical stress occurs, such as an injury or accident, our body responds instantly to protect ourselves by activation of the amygdala. The amygdala is also activated by social stress that triggers emotional reactions. The amydgala responds so fast that we do not become aware of most emotions until we actually notice the reactions in our body, such as trembling, increased heart rate, or sweating. This is so we can react swiftly to danger by fleeing, fighting, freezing, or submitting.

The standard view of the sequence of events that causes emotions used to be: when you see a bear, you feel afraid, and then you run. However, more than 100 years ago, psychologist William James explained that actually we run first and then we feel fear (James, 1884). Joseph Ledoux, in *The Emotional Brain* (1996), points out that the nerve pathways that sense a dangerous situation will send signals to the amygdala within twelve milliseconds. It takes twice as long for the signals to get to the conscious part of the brain (LeDoux, 1996). I often refer to this rapid process as "emotional speed dial," because our bodies can typically react to emotional triggers before we are even aware of the trigger.

Stored forever in the amygdala, emotional memories can trigger physical or emotional responses. I had a patient who as a child lived with an abusive aunt and uncle during the week and stayed with his loving and kind mother on the weekends. When he was married and in his thirties, he noticed that he would get very depressed if his wife worked an evening shift on Sunday, but not if she worked on any other evening. He didn't understand why until we reviewed his history, and then it became clear that the emotional memory he had of leaving his mother on Sundays to return to the abusive aunt and uncle was causing the reaction. Ohman and colleagues showed that fears can be induced without our conscious awareness and that, many years later, we can react to an object or a situation without being aware of the emotions causing the reaction (Ohman, 1992; LeDoux, 1996).

Messages from the Subconscious

In our modern lives, we rarely encounter predators. However, our brains are designed to constantly scan our environment for any signs of danger. When we have significant stresses that remind us of something that caused fear, anger, or guilt earlier in life, our mind will interpret these as dangers. In these situations, our subconscious mind will try to alert us to a problem or protect us from something it perceives as harmful. Unfortunately, our bodies do not use words to tell us that there is a perceived danger. Our bodies just react, often with pain. When we are faced with very stressful situations, especially when we feel trapped and unable to find a solution, our bodies react as if we are in grave danger. The brain will activate the ACC and the ANS, and they can cause tension in certain specific muscles—tension that creates real pain. Over time, the pain can worsen or become widespread. I often use this metaphor to describe this process: "Your body was knocking to let you know that something was bothering you. But you didn't understand it. So, it knocked louder and louder, by creating more pain or new symptoms. When you didn't listen, it rang the doorbell, and finally it threw a rock through a window to get your attention."

An important predictor of whether someone will have successful back surgery is job satisfaction (Gatchel, et. al., 1995). Back pain will often develop in people who are experiencing severe difficulties in their jobs but cannot quit them. Their subconscious mind will often try to "protect" them by causing pain to get them out of the distressing situation. For example, one study found that women who experienced high workloads, little control, and "bullying" in the workplace were more likely to develop fibromyalgia (Kivimaki, et. al., 2004). In the case of Vickie, the woman in chapter 2 with severe headaches, the pain was her body's way of trying to protect her by causing her to leave her job. Despite treatments by many doctors, her headaches lasted for seventeen years until she sought help from this program.

BARRY WAS A THIRTY-FIVE-YEAR-OLD MAN *who had a significant accident while on the job as a firefighter. He was bruised and shaken up, but the doctors found no broken bones when he was seen in the emergency room. The next day, he developed neck pain, and this pain just didn't go away. He had an MRI that showed only mild abnormalities, and his doctors suggested physical therapy. However, that didn't help, and he had to go on disability because he could not work with such severe pain. Over time, he took pain medications and tried to exercise, but nothing helped. After nine months on disability, he came to see me. Barry told me that he had had similar injuries in the past but had always bounced back and had been back at work within a few weeks. It didn't appear that this injury was much different from his other injuries. When I asked if there was something else that might have been different in this situation, he told me that one of his friends had died in the fire. After examining him and finding no evidence of nerve damage in his neck or arms, I explained that he did not have tissue damage in his neck but that the pain was caused by Mind Body Syndrome. I explained that consciously he wanted to return to work but that his nervous system had become sensitized as subconsciously he had feelings of fear, anger, and guilt caused by his friend's death. Barry's pain was real but also curable. He realized that he could get better and started doing the exercises recommended in this book. In three weeks, his pain was 80 percent better. By six weeks, he was back at work.*

The subconscious mind can choose which symptoms occur during times of stress. That is why people who grow up with a parent with headaches will often develop headaches. Someone who grows up with relatives with abdominal pain or back pain will often develop those symptoms decades later. As noted earlier, social contagion is a mechanism by which specific symptoms can be triggered.

Sometimes the way our bodies react can give us a clue to what the mind is trying to tell us. The pain can occur in an appropriate spot—such as the groin pain in the young man after the bachelor's party. When someone develops a pain in the buttocks, there may be someone in their lives who is a "pain in the butt." Someone who develops difficulty swallowing may be reacting to a situation in life that is "hard to swallow." I evaluated a woman with pain in the bottom of her feet. While waiting in line one day, she realized there was a situation in her life that she "just couldn't stand anymore." People often develop headaches before appointments or social situations that are likely to be stressful or where there are people that they have strong feelings about. Often they will be unaware of those strong feelings; they will be subconscious feelings. In fact, emotions are more likely to cause reactions in our bodies when we are unaware that they are influencing us (LeDoux, 1996).

As mentioned in the last chapter, prior learning or priming is also a way in which the subconscious mind chooses a particular symptom. Someone who has injured a certain area is more likely to develop MBS pain in that area because the neurological pattern of pain and nerve sensitization has already been established, and the brain remembers it.

I developed pain shooting down my left arm many years ago during a stressful situation. The pain eventually subsided, but when I get stressed it can reappear for short periods. My brain has not forgotten how to create this particular pain. Now I know what causes it, however, and I can get it to go away by recognizing that I'm stressed about something, dealing with the stress as best I can, and telling my subconscious mind that I don't need the pain to alert me to a dangerous situation or get me out of something that I don't want to do.

Components of the Subconscious Mind

Sigmund Freud was one of the most influential thinkers of the twentieth century. Although several scientists recognized that there was a subconscious part of the mind as early as the mid-1800s (Wilson, 2002), Freud helped us understand many more things about the subconscious. In particular, it has now been conclusively shown that Freud was correct when he proposed these tenets of modern psychology: childhood experiences have powerful effects on personality and later social relationships; we are not aware of most of our thoughts and emotions (they are subconscious); we commonly have conflicting feelings that occur at the same time towards certain individuals or situations; and we frequently act and react to people and situations through subconscious mechanisms (Westen, 1999).

Neuroscientists have now confirmed that the subconscious mind is the major driving force behind almost everything we do on a daily basis. The subconscious mind causes most of us to have mild physical and psychological symptoms on a regular basis, and it can cause some of us to have chronic and serious pain and debilitating symptoms.

Freud also gave us a way of understanding some of the workings of the subconscious mind (Freud and Strachey, 1960). He described an "internal child," which he called the Id (the part of the mind that is selfish, greedy, and only cares about immediate needs, desires, and happiness); an "internal parent," which he named the Superego (the conscience, the part of the mind that wants to be good, to obey, to be liked, to do what it "should"), and an "internal adult," the Ego (the part of the mind mediating conflicts between the internal child's desires and the internal parent's obligations). These descriptions are very helpful in understanding how the mind works to create Mind Body Syndrome.

The Impact of Childhood Hurts

Some children suffer severely from neglect, physical abuse, sexual abuse, or emotional abuse. But every child, even if not overtly abused, gets hurt in some ways. When parents get divorced or argue, when parents are critical or withhold love or give only conditional love, these actions produce pain for their children. Similar reactions can occur in response to taunting or teasing by siblings or other children. One of the most common statements I hear when I evaluate patients is "I never felt loved by my parents," or "I often felt that my father (or mother) would love me only if I acted in certain ways."

Many studies show that childhood hurts lead to an overly sensitive autonomic nervous system in adulthood. In mice, dogs, and monkeys, stressful experiences at an early age cause hyperactivity of the autonomic nervous system, leading to an exaggerated flight, fight, or freeze response (McEwen, 1998). Someone with an overactive autonomic nervous system is more likely to develop Mind Body Syndrome.

Childhood hurts will be remembered in the amygdala, and these emotional memories can be easily and rapidly triggered (on "speed dial") by similar experiences in adults. I saw a man who had a very difficult childhood due to a parental divorce and a father who never took time for him and never showed love for him. When the boy was twelve, his father remarried and sent him to live at a youth home, where he spent the rest of his adolescence. Despite this adversity, he became quite resilient as an adult, found work, and eventually married and had children. He had almost no contact with his father for many years. One day he asked his father, who was visiting the area, to stop by and see his grandchildren. His father came by in a drunken state, stayed only a few minutes, and left. Within a few days, the son developed severe stomach pains, back pain, and anxiety. For years, he sought medical care, never got a clear diagnosis, and ended up taking many different medications without relief. When we met, I told him: "Your father had poured the gasoline for all those years of your childhood, and when you asked him to do something for your children, he lit a match which ignited all the anger and resentment that had built up in your emotional memory. You could handle him neglecting and abusing you, but when he did a similar thing to your children, you had so many strong subconscious feelings that it erupted in your body." In fact, whenever he drank any alcohol after his father's visit, he got violently ill. For those who have had significant traumas in childhood, such as physical, emotional, or sexual abuse; abandonment; bullying; or other obvious difficulties, it is usually easy to identify the relationship between childhood issues and stressors later in life that trigger MBS symptoms.

Often the events that create the emotional priming in childhood are subtle. Fortunately, most people were not exposed to significant emotional, physical, or sexual abuse. In general, those with the greatest number of MBS syndromes are those who have had more significant childhood issues and those who have a very strong "internal parent" (have personality traits of guilt, self-criticism, low self-esteem, high expectations for self, extreme responsibility for others, and self-sacrifice). However, most people have had some form of MBS symptoms occur in their lifetime. Those with less obvious childhood stressors can still develop MBS.

A team of researchers has conducted studies on children whose parents offer love only on a conditional basis. These studies found that people who grow up with parents who give attention and affection only if certain tasks (such as educational or sports achievement, or specific behaviors) are performed were more likely to have low self-esteem, a strong internal parent, and a conflicted relationship with their parents (Assor, et. al., 2004; Roth, et. al., 2009).

Even mild degrees of low self-esteem and the perception of not being good enough can be enough to trigger MBS symptoms. I saw a man who had a sudden onset of severe tinnitus (ringing in the ears) when he was fifty-two years old. He had no history of childhood abuse or neglect and had loving parents. The only childhood hurt we identified was when he moved from a lower-class neighborhood at age ten to a middle-class neighborhood. He was overweight, wore the "wrong" clothes, and got teased by the kids at his new school, which caused him to feel inadequate and embarrassed. He had no symptoms at all until he was twenty-seven years old, when he had an anxiety attack while working at a church on a project. He was a new member of this church, which he felt to be more prestigious than his old church. He was trying to fit in and be accepted. Years later, at age fifty-two, his ears started ringing just days before Thanksgiving, a day when he and his wife always went to her mother's house for dinner. He told me that his mother-in-law "never liked me, never accepted me, never thought I was good enough for her daughter." It became clear that his symptoms were a reactivation of a subtle childhood hurt—not being accepted in his new neighborhood—that had lived in his emotional memory for all those years.

Careful questioning and evaluation will almost always lead to a clear understanding of the causes of MBS, if you pay close attention to childhood events and how those can get triggered in adolescence or adulthood. I have interviewed hundreds of people with MBS and, so far, there have been only two people for whom the source of their symptoms did not become clear to both me and the patient after an in-depth interview.

Childhood hurts affect the internal child, and it will react with anger, resentment, and fear to traumatic experiences and stressful events. Powerless to change their situation, children will store those hurts and emotions in the amygdala. When they become adolescents and adults, stressful events can easily reignite these emotions.

The Role of Conscience

The internal parent is the conscience within the subconscious mind and expects us to perform our obligations and duties. This part of the mind is the seat of guilt, shame, humiliation, self-criticism, self-blame, the need to be liked, the need to be good, high self-expectations, low self-esteem, and perfectionism. Those who grew up with a strong conscience are less likely to speak up for themselves and assert themselves. They are more likely to do many things for others and neglect doing things for themselves. They are often people who are shy and reserved, who don't like to draw attention to themselves, and who tend to hold emotions in. People with MBS almost always have many of these characteristics and emotions. Some families, some cultures, and even some religions teach children to emphasize these characteristics early in life. Many of my patients grew up in religions that tend to emphasize guilt and self-criticism. I rarely see people who are selfish and narcissistic in this program. Rather, it is the "good and kind" people of the world who tend to suffer with Mind Body Syndrome.

The subconscious mind is likely to produce physical symptoms at times of severe stress as an escape mechanism for the buildup of emotions that have no other outlet. A woman developed back pain when she was called on to care for her ailing mother, who had always been demanding and critical of her. Her conflict was between the moral obligation she felt to her mother and the anger and resentment toward her that started in childhood. She also felt guilty about resenting the work she had to do for her mother. She felt trapped, and that created tremendous tension in the mind. For her and many of my patients, the mind is like a pressure cooker, and there is often no outlet for these strong feelings. In the face of this tremendous conflict within the mind, the conscience will often not even allow these feelings to come into consciousness. These strong subconscious feelings were perceived by the brain as danger signals that were expressed as back pain.

In addition to earlier emotional events and the presence of personality traits of guilt, self-criticism, or needing to please, a third key element in the development of MBS is perceived (and often real) powerlessness. Most of the time when MBS symptoms develop, there is a feeling of being trapped in some way. It may be that one is trapped in a job with a very difficult boss or backbiting colleagues. I saw a woman who felt trapped in a difficult marriage who had severe knee pain for a year. When the marriage was finally dissolved, her knee pain disappeared. Another way to be trapped is to be unable to express one's deep feelings. I think of this as being "verbally" trapped, when there are no close friends or relatives to whom one can disclose emotions. Many times, the emotions and situations causing MBS symptoms are so shameful or unacceptable or trigger so much guilt that the feelings are kept hidden by the subconscious mind. Those who feel trapped and tend to be unable to speak up for themselves are likely to suppress feelings of anger or resentment.

Any of these strong feelings and conflicts within the mind can easily create physical symptoms. I recently worked with a woman who had severe fibromyalgia pain that disappeared after taking this program. When I asked her the most important thing that she did to help herself, she told me that she had finally decided to stand up for herself, to not let everyone "walk all over her," and to make some decisions to do things she wanted to do, rather than continually accede to others' desires.

The Role of Gender

Women are more likely than men to have MBS. Many more women than men have migraine headaches, TMJ pain, and fibromyalgia, and women have slightly more back pain. The reason has eluded explanation for many years. If one understands how MBS develops, it appears that there are several potential explanations. First, women are more likely to be socialized to be deferential and take care of the needs of others before attending to their own needs. They are also more likely to be the victims of abuse. Women are more often in employment positions that are subservient and at the same time are expected to be sexy and beautiful, as well as manage most of the duties in the home. They are also more likely to be in situations where they are caring for children, for aging parents, or for grandparents.

Women are more likely to be oriented toward wanting to please others and feel like they should be better or do more, and they are less likely to assert themselves. Men are more likely to be assertive and blame others rather than themselves for problems in their lives. In fact, two very large studies of men and women around the world showed that women are more likely to be conscientious and agreeable and to worry than are men. Surprisingly, these differences are greater in North America and Europe than in countries with more traditional cultures (Costa, et. al., 2001; Schmitt et. al., 2008).

Obviously, men also get MBS, and many men have endured childhood hurts and have very strong feelings of obligation and guilt and other indications of a highly developed conscience. One thing that I often tell people is that the reason that they have Mind Body Syndrome is not that they are weak or crazy or incompetent—it is because they are human. Because of how we are constructed, the interaction between the mind and body frequently causes the body to react to thoughts and feelings.

Mind Body Syndrome and Health Care

In 1976, the social critic Ivan Illich warned of the potential iatrogenic consequences of labeling diseases: that the medical profession can actually make people sick (Illich, 1976). When patients with MBS are labeled as having degenerative disc disease on the basis of an MRI or as having "fibromyalgia" because they have widespread body pain, symptoms can be exacerbated and patients harmed by medical diagnoses.

Yet there is also danger in certain diagnoses often given by some "alternative" medical practitioners, such as chronic yeast infection and adrenal fatigue. Such diagnoses can have effects similar to traditional medical labeling, turning a person with MBS symptoms that are due to stress and emotions into a patient with a condition that needs to be treated by herbal remedies or other interventions.

Most people have physical and psychological symptoms on a regular basis due to psychological states, and a tremendous amount of money is spent on the diagnosis and treatment of disorders that are manifestations of Mind Body Syndrome. If MBS were widely recognized by the lay public and medical professionals—both traditional and alternative practitioners—many people's symptoms could be alleviated, we would spend much less on health care, and we could prevent people from developing chronic symptom complexes that can cause tremendous suffering for decades.

The treatment of these disorders requires taking a careful history, judicious use of diagnostic tests to rule out serious pathological processes, attention to past and current psychosocial stressors and reactions to these stressors, validation of the real nature of the symptoms, explanation of the psycho-physiological basis of the symptoms, and brief educational and psychological interventions. In these ways, patients are empowered to gain control over their symptoms, understand themselves better, and acquire tools to improve their psychological state.

The Psychology of Mind Body Syndrome

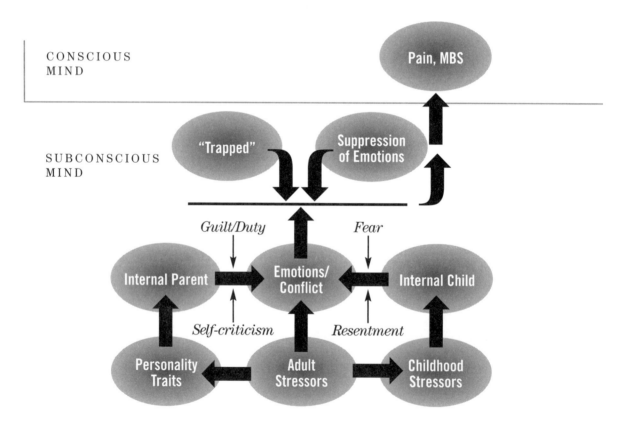

HOW MBS DEVELOPS FROM THE PSYCHOLOGICAL POINT OF VIEW: Childhood and adult stressors trigger feelings of fear, anger, or resentment, which are stored in emotional memory (internal child). Personality traits learned in childhood create a strong sense of duty, self-blame, self-criticism, guilt, and excessive concern for others (internal parent). In situations where people feel trapped by stressful events that trigger emotions from childhood hurts, or feel a conflict between what they want for themselves and what they feel they need to do for others, MBS symptoms are likely to develop, especially if there is no outlet to express these feelings or the feelings are actively suppressed.

chapter 5

Do You Have Mind Body Syndrome?

It is more important to know what sort of person has the disease than what kind of disease the person has. — Hippocrates

How do you know if your pain or other symptoms are the result of Mind Body Syndrome? First, you need to rule out tissue breakdown disorders that require biomedical treatments. If you have had complete testing and no serious medical or physical disorder was found—no fractures, no cancer, no heart disease, no infections, no nerve damage, no clear tissue pathology—then you very likely have MBS.

Mind Body Syndrome does not cause cancer or heart disease or stroke. These are conditions that increase in the population with increasing age and cause significant illness and, of course, often death. These diseases are obviously tissue breakdown disorders, and there is no clear evidence that they can be cured by changing how one thinks. I recommend biomedical treatment for people with these disorders. This program is not designed for people with this category of disorders, although it may help cope with common reactions to these disorders, such as anxiety or depression.

There is another group of disorders that I do not consider to be a part of MBS. Representative disorders in this category include asthma, systemic lupus, rheumatoid arthritis, and multiple sclerosis. Although these disorders occur in younger people (as does MBS), these are also clearly tissue break-down disorders. It has been shown that stress and emotional reactions to stress can exacerbate these medical conditions. Since these conditions have a physical basis in the body, if I encourage people with these conditions to take this program, it is not to cure their disorder, but to prevent their symptoms from worsening. I also recommend continuing their medical treatments as well.

This program is designed for those with MBS, those in whom there is no tissue breakdown process in the body, whose pain and other MBS symptoms are caused by stress and emotional reactions to stress. For such people, this program can offer the opportunity for a cure or a remission of symptoms.

Those who can be certain of having MBS are those who have been diagnosed with tension headaches, migraine headaches, neck pain, back pain, whiplash, fibromyalgia, irritable bowel syndrome, chronic fatigue syndrome, interstitial cystitis, insomnia, tinnitus, chronic abdominal or pelvic pain, or any other of the common MBS syndromes listed in the table in chapter 2. However, since MBS is so common and because the ANS fibers send nerves to literally every part of the body, there are many people with MBS who have pain and other symptoms that may not be included on this list. A careful medical review is necessary for everyone with chronic symptoms to rule out a serious medical condition. If you are suffering from chronic symptoms that your doctors have been unable to diagnose or treat, you may have MBS, even if your symptoms are not listed in the table. If the true diagnosis remains in doubt, you should seek consultation with me or one of the other doctors who are knowledgeable about MBS and who have experience in diagnosing this condition. A list of such doctors is included in the Appendix.

Illustrative Stories

To prepare you for the kind of self-evaluation you will be doing, here are some cases I have encountered that illustrate some common patterns seen in the development of MBS.

A FORTY-FIVE-YEAR-OLD WOMAN *developed stomach pains and anxiety attacks in the fall one year after her husband died. He was terminally ill and, in accord with his wishes, she had to decide to disconnect his life support, which she felt was in conflict with her religious beliefs. Each fall, her pains returned and increased. Several GI specialists saw her, but no one could help her resolve her pain. Through this program, she learned that her feelings about her husband's death (primarily guilt and loss) caused her pain. Her anxiety attacks were generally in the afternoon, occuring almost exactly at the time of day that he died.*

A FIFTY-TWO-YEAR-OLD MAN *developed back pain while on a plane from Michigan to California, where he was living. As a child, his father was his hero and well liked by everyone in his small Michigan town. His mother was critical and self-absorbed. She demeaned the young boy constantly, and one day he replied to her in a disrespectful manner at home. Later that day, the mother called the local police and had him taken out of school in handcuffs and put into the town jail for the rest of the day, simply for talking back to his mother. After growing up, he moved to California. When he was fifty, he returned home to visit his father, who was now elderly and in a nursing home. Upon arriving home, he found that his mother was mistreating his father and he felt that his father was "imprisoned" in the nursing home. On the flight back, he developed severe back pains that lasted for 2 years.*

A THIRTY-FOUR-YEAR-OLD MAN *was raised by a dominant father and a submissive mother in a small, very religious town. He was highly skilled in school and sports, and was admired by most people. When drunk, his father would often physically abuse his mother, but this was accepted as "normal" in his community and no action was ever taken. When asked how he felt about this, the patient replied that he often vowed that if he ever hit a woman, he would "cut off his hand." When he was a Ph.D. student, he was under the stress of preparing for his oral exams and was working feverishly on a big project. At this time, he began to have pain in both of his hands. The pain progressed to the point where he could not turn a doorknob, could not work on a computer, and could not pick up his infant son. Despite extensive testing and seeking care from several hand specialists, no one could explain his pain. When asked to recall any other events that occurred at the time of the onset of his pain, he noted that there was a conflict between two of his mentors. One mentor was a woman, who began to tell people that he was not fit to be in the Ph.D. program. He felt that she threatened his ability to complete his program. He was unaware of the depth of anger he felt towards her and his even stronger feelings of guilt at the prospect of his anger towards a woman. This internal and subconscious conflict was the trigger for his severe hand pain.*

The specific symptoms caused by MBS can be quite different, even though the stressor and the emotional reaction may be very similar to that which occurred in childhood, as shown by the following brief vignettes.

A TEENAGER DEVELOPED HEADACHES *after being sexually abused by an older brother. She developed fibromyalgia later in life at a time when she was emotionally abused by her husband.*

A WOMAN DEVELOPED MIGRAINE HEADACHES *as a child after her parents divorced and then developed interstitial cystitis as an adult after her own divorce.*

Sometimes MBS symptoms can be triggered by a positive event. In my own life, I developed neck pain after my daughter was born. She was our first child, and I was extremely happy at the time. However, her arrival complicated our lives. I was busy with work and busy at home, and my daughter didn't sleep well at night. I was up several times a night with her, walking up and down the stairs with her to get her back to sleep. After several months of this, my wife and I disagreed on how to deal with her crying at night. Now, in retrospect, I realize I felt stressed, resentful, and trapped. Not being able to express (or even recognize) these feelings, I developed neck pain, which persisted for several months.

In a minority of people with MBS, their early childhood experiences did not create the emotional events that typically lead to priming of the ANS. Those with loving, stable families and happy childhoods are less likely to develop MBS later in life. However, they are primed to expect that these relationships will continue, and when something happens that tears their world apart, MBS can develop.

A FORTY-TWO-YEAR-OLD WOMAN *grew up in a nurturing, close family within an idyllic rural community. Her mother chose to give her a larger share of the family inheritance, and this set off a contested will and the loss of her close relationships with her siblings. The trauma of those changes was enough to trigger severe back pain.*

Mind Body Syndrome Self-Diagnosis

To figure out if you have MBS and what issues in your life may have contributed to this disorder, take the time to complete the work sheets below. They will help you understand yourself better, and this understanding is the key to ridding yourself of your pain. This section is based upon the detailed interview I use with my patients.

STEP 1: SYMPTOMS

The following list of symptoms and diagnoses are likely to be caused by MBS (though some of them can also be caused by other medical conditions that can be easily ruled out by your physician). The more of these you have had during your lifetime, the more likely it is that you have MBS. People with several of these conditions have usually seen many doctors and been given multiple diagnoses, but their doctors have not considered MBS. This is because biotechnological medical practice tends to look at each body system in isolation. You may have seen a neurologist, orthopedic surgeon or neurosurgeon, gastroenterologist, rheumatologist, or others. But no one is looking at the whole person. MBS occurs in people, not in body parts, and we can only understand it by evaluating the whole person, the mind, and the body.

It is very common for MBS symptoms to start in childhood or adolescence. Many people develop headaches, stomach aches, dizziness, fatigue, anxiety, or other symptoms while they are young and then later in life develop back or neck pain, fibromyalgia, irritable bowel syndrome, or other conditions.

CHECK EACH ITEM ON THIS LIST and write down at what age you were when each set of symptoms first appeared in your life.

Date of onset:

Date of onset:

1. Heartburn, acid reflux _____
2. Abdominal pains _____
3. Irritable bowel syndrome _____
4. Tension headaches _____
5. Migraine headaches _____
6. Unexplained rashes _____
7. Anxiety and/or panic attacks

_____
8. Depression _____

9. Obsessive-compulsive thought patterns

_____
10. Eating disorders _____
11. Insomnia or trouble sleeping _____
12. Fibromyalgia _____
13. Back pain _____
14. Neck pain _____
15. Shoulder pain _____
16. Repetitive stress injury _____

Date of onset:

17. Carpal tunnel syndrome _____
18. Reflex sympathetic dystrophy (RSD) _____
19. Temporomandibular joint syndrome (TMJ) _____
20. Chronic tendonitis _____
21. Facial pain _____
22. Numbness, tingling sensations _____
23. Fatigue or chronic fatigue syndrome _____
24. Palpitations _____

Date of onset:

25. Chest pain _____
26. Hyperventilation _____
27. Interstitial cystitis/spastic bladder (irritable bladder syndrome) _____
28. Pelvic pain _____
29. Muscle tenderness _____
30. Postural orthostatic tachycardia syndrome (POTS) _____
31. Tinnitus _____
32. Dizziness _____
33. PTSD _____

STEP 2: INVESTIGATE YOUR CHILDHOOD

Now consider the following questions and write brief answers to as many of them as seem important.

What words would you use to describe your father?

(Substitute another caregiver if you didn't grow up with your father.)

_____
_____
_____

What kind of work did your father do? Was he successful in his career?

_____

Was your father loving? Did he hug you or tell you he loved you? Was he supportive?

_____
_____

Were you particularly close to your father? Did he confide in you?

_____

Was his love conditional?

_____

Did your father have high expectations of you?

_____

Was he critical or judgmental?

_____

Was he a perfectionist?

_____

Did he yell at you?

_____

Did he hit or punish you?

_____

Were you afraid of him?

_____

Was your father aloof, neglectful, or self-centered?

_____

Were some children given preferential treatment or treated more harshly than others?
If so, how did that make you feel? How did that affect the relationship between you and any of
your siblings?

_____

_____

Did your father drink or use drugs? If so, how did that affect him, the family, and you?

_____

Did your father have any mental health issues?

_____

Was he anxious, worried, or insecure?

_____

How did your father treat your mother?

_____

Did you identify with your father?

_____

Did you attempt to be like him or to be different from him?

_____

What words would you use to describe your mother (or another caregiver)?

_____

_____

_____

What kind of work did your mother do?

_____

Was she successful in her career?

_____

Was your mother loving? Did she hug you or tell you she loved you? Was she supportive?

_____

_____

Were you particularly close to your mother? Did she confide in you?

_____

Was her love conditional?

_____

Did your mother have high expectations of you?

_____

Was she critical or judgmental?

_____

Was she a perfectionist?

_____

Did she yell at you?

_____

Did she hit or punish you?

_____

Were you afraid of her?

_____

Was your mother aloof, neglectful, or self-centered?

_____

Were some children given preferential treatment or treated more harshly than others?
If so, how did that make you feel? How did that affect the relationship between you and any of
your siblings?

_____

_____

Did your mother drink or use drugs? If so, how did that affect her, the family, and you?

_____

Did your mother have any mental health issues?

_____

Was she anxious, worried, or insecure?

_____

Did you identify with your mother?

_____

Did you attempt to be like her or to be different from her?

_____

How did your mother treat your father?

_____

Who was in charge of the house?

_____

Who handled disciplinary issues?

_____

Did your parents argue?

_____

Did anyone other than your mother and father have responsibility for you or care for you as a child?
If so, who?

_____

Repeat the above questions for these individuals if they had significant roles in your upbringing.
Use separate paper for these questions.

Think of the relationships you had with your siblings while you were growing up.

Were there resentments or jealousies?

_____

_____

Was there any cruelty, meanness, or abuse?

_____

Did any of your siblings have any illnesses, psychological problems, or drug abuse problems?

_____

Did any of your siblings rebel, act out, or behave in ways that were upsetting to your parents or to you?

_____

How did you react to these situations?

_____

How was money handled in your family?

_____

Did you feel that money was a scarce resource?

_____

Did your parents use money as a controlling agent?

_____

Were they generous with money or not?

_____

Did you work as a child or teenager?

_____

Finally, consider if there were any particularly stressful or traumatic events in your childhood.

Describe any of the following: deaths, moves, bullying, taunting, teasing, emotional or physical abuse, changes in school situations, conflicts with teachers, or changes in family situations?

_____

_____

_____

_____

_____

_____

_____

_____

_____

_____

_____

Have you ever been subjected to any episodes of unwanted sexual activity or sexual abuse?

_____

_____

_____

_____

Childhood experiences create very powerful reactions in our minds that remain for the rest of our lives. Emotions that are generated when we are young can very easily get triggered later in life, and, when they are triggered, can cause the start of Mind Body Syndrome. It is usually relatively easy to identify the childhood issues that people with MBS have grown up with.

It is well known that a large percentage of the people with irritable bowel syndrome, fibromyalgia, TMJ syndrome, and other MBS illnesses have been neglected or abused—sexually, emotionally, or physically—as children or adolescents. People who have suffered from severe childhood abuse are most likely to have many forms of MBS.

I saw a woman whose mother was a prostitute and a cocaine addict and whose father was a heroin addict who sexually abused and even tortured her. She became a prostitute and a cocaine addict as an adolescent. She eventually went to jail, broke her addiction to drugs, and was able to raise a daughter and find a job. However, over all those years of traumatic experiences, she developed fibromyalgia, migraine headaches, irritable bowel syndrome, TMJ syndrome, chronic fatigue, back pain, insomnia, anxiety, depression, and several other MBS disorders.

Not everyone with MBS has had severe childhood traumas, however. For many people, the childhood issues that generate strong emotions are normal childhood experiences. How many of us have felt jealous of a sibling or ostracized by friends in middle school or picked on by a bully in elementary school? These common experiences can also generate enough emotions to cause

MBS syndrome, either at the time of the events or, more commonly, later in life.

I treated a woman who grew up with loving parents but with a difficult younger sister. Her sister was constantly in trouble, and my patient was always covering up for her, even though she resented her sister lying and avoiding responsibilities. When my patient was thirty-three years old, she was leading a team at work in an important project. One woman on the team avoided her share of the work and tried to cover up her lack of effort. My patient was trapped in a situation eerily similar to that of dealing with her younger sister and had to double her work to get the project completed. During that time, she developed back pain because the situation at work triggered the stored emotional reactions from her youth. Several years later, she developed headaches every time she drove across town to visit her father, who was in a nursing home that her sister had selected for its proximity to her. After learning of her life story, it became clear that her resentment of her sister was the underlying trigger for the back pain and headaches.

STEP 3: CORE ISSUES

Once you have carefully and honestly reviewed the stresses in your life, you will likely begin to see patterns. You will be able to identify your "core issues," those issues that have been stored in your subconscious mind and that are most likely to trigger the onset of physical and psychological symptoms. Indicate which of the following patterns apply to you, or describe any other patterns that apply to you.

1. Loss and abandonment (losing a parent or sibling, divorce, moving) _____

2. Childhood abuse or neglect (physical, sexual, emotional abuse; never feeling loved or cared for) _____

3. Not fitting in or feeling ostracized (being teased or picked on, being shy and reserved, not being athletic or popular) _____

4. Feeling pressure to succeed or be perfect (from parents, other family members, church or religious organizations, or self) _____

5. Feeling inferior to siblings or other relatives (not as beautiful, funny, athletic, interesting, accomplished) _____

6. Never feeling good enough, having to "earn" love from parents, feeling criticized much of the time _____

7. Resentment and/or anger towards family members, religious leaders, neighbors _____

8. Learning to be anxious, worried, or insecure _____

9. Identifying with one or several family members and trying to emulate them; trying to be different from one or several family members _____

10. Other patterns _____

_____

_____

_____

STEP 4: PERSONALITY TRAITS

These factors are commonly seen in people with MBS. Check those that apply to you. Would you describe yourself as:

1. Having low self-esteem _____

2. Being a perfectionist _____

3. Having high expectations of yourself _____

4. Wanting to be good and/or be liked _____

5. Frequently feeling guilt _____

6. Feeling dependent on others _____

7. Being conscientious _____

8. Being hard on yourself _____

9. Being overly responsible _____

10. Taking on responsibility for others _____

11. Often worrying _____

12. Having difficulty making decisions _____

13. Following rules strictly _____

14. Having difficulty letting go _____

15. Feeling cautious, shy, or reserved _____

16. Tending to hold thoughts and feelings in _____

17. Tending to harbor rage or resentment _____

18. Not standing up for yourself _____

Conflict in one's mind is a very important part of the mechanism that creates and perpetuates MBS. The traits above are aspects of the conscience—they are things that we feel obligated to do or ways we feel obligated to be. Most people with MBS are people who try hard, who care what others think of them, who want to be good and want to be liked. They tend to be conscientious, responsible, and hard on themselves. These personality traits are generally found in good people, people you would like to know and be friends with. The problem is that people like this put extra pressure on themselves. They tend to get down on themselves and beat themselves up for their failings. When external events and stressors occur and we compound the stress by putting more pressure on ourselves, we are much more likely to develop MBS.

STEP 5: FINDING CONNECTIONS BETWEEN LIFE STRESSES, CORE ISSUES, AND THE ONSET OF MBS SYMPTOMS

Once you have identified your core issues, review the list of potential MBS symptoms above. On the next page, list the times in your life when you developed any of the MBS manifestations in chronological order. Think carefully about what events occurred just prior to or during the onset of symptoms. You will typically find that the symptoms began at or shortly after you experienced something that was stressful and that reminded you of your core issues (triggering your emotional speed dial), and you felt trapped in that situation. List each symptom, then write down the triggering events or situations, and the emotions and/or core issues which caused the symptoms to occur.

When you place the symptoms and diagnoses that have occurred next to the life stressors, see what patterns emerge and what connections you can make. This is a critical step in figuring out why you have MBS. Do this for each of your MBS symptoms. For each symptom, think carefully about what was going on in your life at the time this symptom began. What events had occurred that bothered you? What emotions did you feel? How were these events or emotions similar to those you experienced in childhood? Which core issues might have been triggered? Did you feel trapped in some way, either physically or verbally?

Be as open and honest as you can in this process. Often it is very obvious that stressful life events in childhood have created the emotional memories of hurt, loss, fear, guilt, or anger, and it is equally obvious that certain stressors later in life triggered MBS symptoms.

However, sometimes it takes a fair amount of introspection and searching to find the connections. It is common for mild stressors in adult life to trigger significant symptoms if the stressor is related to earlier stressors, particularly from childhood. Neglect or lack of love by a parent can create a childhood hurt that can get triggered later in life by seemingly mild interactions.

Age	MBS symptom(s) (from Step 1)	Potential triggering events	Emotions that were triggered/core issues
____	_____	_____	_____
____	_____	_____	_____
____	_____	_____	_____
____	_____	_____	_____
____	_____	_____	_____
____	_____	_____	_____
____	_____	_____	_____
____	_____	_____	_____
____	_____	_____	_____
____	_____	_____	_____
____	_____	_____	_____
____	_____	_____	_____
____	_____	_____	_____
____	_____	_____	_____
____	_____	_____	_____
____	_____	_____	_____
____	_____	_____	_____
____	_____	_____	_____
____	_____	_____	_____
____	_____	_____	_____
____	_____	_____	_____
____	_____	_____	_____
____	_____	_____	_____
____	_____	_____	_____

Making Your Decision

For many people, doing these exercises will make it clear to you that you do have MBS. If you can see the connections between your life experiences and your symptoms, your chances of curing your pain are very good. You are now ready to begin the powerful program contained in the rest of this book.

One young woman I evaluated had experienced severe childhood traumas and consequently had developed a very long list of disorders, including iritable bowel syndrome, anxiety, depression, neck pain, TMJ disorder, and fibromyalgia. She had been treated unsuccessfully for many years and was convinced that she was in a hopeless situation. After reviewing the clear connections between her life events and the onset of her MBS symptoms, she suddenly looked up at me and said, "I have Mind Body Syndrome." The certainty and confidence in her voice were striking, as she realized at that moment that she could take control of her life and shed these disorders that seemed incurable.

However, if you're not sure if you have MBS, or that your life experiences are actually the cause of your pain, consider these steps:

- Make sure you have seen a doctor and that you have had enough testing to rule out a purely physical cause for your pain and/or other symptoms.

- Discuss these issues with a counselor, relative, or good friend to help uncover the connections between the stresses in your life and your symptoms.

- Do further reading. I recommend reading John Sarno's landmark book, *The Mindbody Prescription*. Dr. Sarno is a pioneer in this field, and this book describes how the MBS syndrome works (his term for it is Tension Myositis Syndrome). There are a number of other useful books listed in the appendix, such as David Clarke's *They Can't Find Anything Wrong*, and Nancy Selfridge's *Freedom From Fibromyalgia*.

- See a doctor or psychologist who specializes in MBS. There is a list of such people in the Appendix. If you would like to make an appointment with me, you can contact me on my website: www.unlearnyourpain.com.

Once you have the correct diagnosis and you can say to yourself, "I have Mind Body Syndrome," you are ready to use the rest of this book to heal yourself. If you participate in this program, it is very likely that you will reduce or eliminate your MBS symptoms, increase your understanding of yourself, and learn how to gain control and mastery over your mind and body. In fact, the program has been so helpful to so many people that most people who have taken the program recommend it to everyone they know, including those who do not have symptoms of MBS.

chapter 6

Starting the Program: The Power Is in Your Hands

You never find yourself until you face the truth. — Pearl Bailey

To be nobody—but yourself—in a world which is doing its best, night and day, to make you everybody else—means to fight the hardest battle which any human being can fight; and never stop fighting. — e. e. cummings

The remainder of this book consists of a guide to curing yourself of Mind Body Syndrome. It is based upon the live, in-person course that I teach to individuals with MBS and is therefore designed to be completed in four weeks. However, one advantage of completing the program in book form is that you can do the exercises at your own pace.

This program is designed for those who have MBS. As mentioned before, it is not designed for those with pain or other symptoms caused by cancer, fractures, infections, or inflammatory diseases. Symptoms caused by MBS can be cured by doing this program and taking it seriously. The most important factors in getting better are the belief that you do, in fact, have Mind Body Syndrome and understanding what factors in your life have caused the stresses and emotions that have triggered the symptoms of MBS. It is my experience that those who do not have this belief and these understandings have a much more difficult time in ridding themselves of MBS. If you have significant doubts about whether your symptoms are caused by MBS, consider the advice given at the end of chapter 5.

Once you are convinced that you have MBS, I invite you to continue with this book. The program is detailed and comprehensive. It will guide you in a step-by-step process of removing the barriers to getting better. I expect that three things will happen by taking this course. First, you will learn to understand yourself much better. Second, you will see significant improvement or cure of your physical symptoms. Finally, you will gain more mastery and control over your emotions and your life.

Components of the Program

The program consists of six "Rs" for curing MBS. These are reading about MBS, repudiation of the physical explanations for your symptoms, writing exercises, reflecting with meditative exercises, reprogramming your mind, and rebuilding your life. You have already taken the first step, reading or learning enough about MBS so that you are convinced that you do have MBS and that you can be helped by this program.

The second step is actively rejecting any diagnoses for symptoms actually caused by MBS that you may have been given by doctors who are unfamiliar with MBS. It is very important to take this step. You must have a clear understanding that your back pain is not caused by a bulging disc or spinal stenosis; that your abdominal pain is not caused by irritable bowel syndrome; that your headaches are not caused by migraines; that your whole-body pain is not caused by fibromyalgia; that your jaw pain is not caused by TMJ syndrome. Even though these diagnoses may help to explain your symptoms and validate them as "real," they are not helpful in terms of curing your symptoms. Of course, I am not asking you to repudiate physical disorders such as hypothyroidism, rheumatoid arthritis, cancer, or heart disease.

It is absolutely true that your symptoms are real; they are not imagined or just in your head. The symptoms are in the mind and body, are caused by a set of learned nerve connections that have been sensitized, and are caused by Mind Body Syndrome. I have found that it is critical to be able to state clearly and forcefully, "I have Mind Body Syndrome, and I can cure myself." This is always the first thing I do in every class that I teach. We go around the room, and each person is asked the question: What is your diagnosis?

For the first exercise in this program, I invite you to do the following. Repeat the following sentence to yourself silently. "I have Mind Body Syndrome, and I can cure myself." Now repeat it to yourself out loud. Now do it more loudly and forcefully. Say it again with determination and belief that you will get better. Say it with a smile on your face, knowing that you are on the road to getting better. Say it to members of your family, to your friends, to anyone who is a support for you. There should be no shame in saying this, because you understand that everyone has MBS to some degree at some time in their life. I have it, and I even continue to get occasional symptoms now in response to emotions. That is our human condition; that is how our minds and bodies were made. The more you are able to be open with yourself and others about MBS, and the more you are able to accept the diagnosis as the true underlying source of your symptoms, the quicker you will be able to get better.

Why does this program work so well? The reason we see such rapid and complete responses is that the program attacks the underlying cause of MBS, which is the painful nerve connections that have been learned by the mind and the body. When you repeat the sentence "I have MBS, and I can cure myself," you are activating the dorso-lateral prefrontal cortex (DLPFC). The DLPFC inactivates the anterior cingulate cortex (ACC) and interrupts the vicious circle of nerves, involving the amygdala and the autonomic nervous system, which creates the symptoms of MBS. These nerve connections are located in the subconscious part of the brain, and by repeating this sentence you are using the conscious part of the brain (DLPFC) to override the MBS pathways. The rest of the program does the same thing. The writing, reflecting, reprogramming, and rebuilding exercises are all designed to activate the conscious portions of the brain to help you unlearn your pain.

Studies by Kirsch (1985) and Bandura (1997) have demonstrated that people who expect that they will improve and those who believe that they have the ability to master their situations (known as self-efficacy) are much more likely to get better. I believe that each and every person with Mind Body Syndrome can get better because it is possible to overcome MBS by using this program. Those people who are unable to accept that their symptoms are due to MBS, or who do not develop positive expectations of relief, or who are unable to believe that they can make changes in their health and in their lives are the people who are less likely to improve.

A Commitment to Heal

This program will require about an hour of work each day, which is obviously a large commitment. I urge you to do this program wholeheartedly and diligently. However, there are a few caveats. As I mentioned above, you can do this program at your own pace. If it takes you more than four weeks, that is perfectly fine. Feel free to decide what is best for you. Taking on a large commitment at a time when you are extremely busy can be stressful in itself, and my intention is not to add more stress to your life. As I noted in chapter 4, many people who have MBS are high achievers or perfectionists. They are likely to be hard on themselves and "beat themselves up" for not reaching their goals. Do not fall into the trap of working too hard on this program, and do not get down on yourself if you miss doing the homework on one or more days. You will have success in this program, but don't create unnecessary worry by putting too much pressure on yourself.

The most important single piece of advice that I can give you is: Be kind to yourself. There are enough stressors in the world and in your life. Don't put more pressure on yourself. Don't increase your guilt or self-blame or self-criticism. These are factors that create MBS and can prevent its cure. Take it easy on yourself. Don't beat yourself up. Don't worry if you don't see improvements immediately. Continue to do the exercises in this program. If you do, you will benefit, and the people in your life will benefit. Most people with MBS do not take enough time for themselves and don't do enough for themselves.

In summary, it is critical that you believe that you have MBS and that you can be cured. It is critical that you take the time to do the program wholeheartedly. And it is critical to be kind to yourself as you take these four weeks to improve your health and your life.

chapter 7

Week One: Taking Control of Your Life

I have much ado to know myself. — William Shakespeare

I need to move, I need to wake up, I need to change, I need to shake up.
I need to speak out, something's got to break up, I've been asleep, and
I need to wake up. Now. — Melissa Etheridge

During the first week, you will learn important skills that you will use during the rest of the program. You will have these skills for the rest of your life. This chapter will introduce you to the writing, reflecting, and reprogramming the mind exercises that are the basis of the MBS program. Make sure that you have set aside about an hour a day, either in one block or in two half-hour time periods. The time you take for yourself will change your life.

Writing Away Your Pain

Many of the writing exercises in this program are based on insights from the therapeutic journaling movement and specifically on the excellent research of James Pennebaker (1990 and 2004). Dr. Pennebaker has shown that writing about stressful situations allows people to become healthier, develop perspective, and learn to let go of the reactions that have imprisoned them. He has also developed some specific writing activities that help do that, some of which we have incorporated into this program. We call them the Write Away Process, because you will be writing away your pain.

The first week's writing exercise is called the 25-Minute Jog. I suggest that you complete one of these "jogs" each day.

You will need to create three lists to guide your writing for this week. Two are lists of stressful events in your life, and the third consists of some of your personality traits that may be contributing to MBS.

Creating Your Lists: Stressors and Personality Traits

List of past traumatic or stressful events: Include any interactions or events which caused hurt, shame, resentment, embarrassment, pain, anger, guilt, humiliation, fear, worry, or other negative emotions. Try to think of anything and everything which falls into this category and list each event or situation as a separate item. Include events from your childhood as far back as you can remember. While you're doing this exercise, put down anything that comes into your mind, even if you think it may have no connection to your MBS symptoms. **Ignore the lines with the minus and plus signs for now.**

a. _____

    − _____

    + _____

b. _____

    − _____

    + _____

c. _____

    − _____

    + _____

d. _____

    − _____

    + _____

e. _____

    − _____

    + _____

f. _____

    − _____

    + _____

g. _____

    – _____

    + _____

h. _____

    – _____

    + _____

i. _____

    – _____

    + _____

j. _____

    – _____

    + _____

k. _____

    – _____

    + _____

l. _____

    – _____

    + _____

m. _____

    – _____

    + _____

n. _____

    – _____

    + _____

o. _____

    – _____

    + _____

p. _____

    – _____

    + _____

q. _____

    − _____

    + _____

r. _____

    − _____

    + _____

s. _____

    − _____

    + _____

t. _____

    − _____

    + _____

u. _____

    − _____

    + _____

v. _____

    − _____

    + _____

w. _____

    − _____

    + _____

x. _____

    − _____

    + _____

y. _____

    − _____

    + _____

z. _____

    − _____

    + _____

List of current stressors: Include any interactions or events which cause hurt, shame, resentment, embarrassment, pain, anger, guilt, humiliation, fear, worry, or other emotions. Try to think of anything and everything which falls into this category and list each event or situation as a separate item. While you're doing this exercise, put down anything that comes into your mind, even if you think it may have no connection to your MBS symptoms. **Ignore the lines with the minus and plus signs for now.**

a. _____

    − _____

    + _____

b. _____

    − _____

    + _____

c. _____

    − _____

    + _____

d. _____

    − _____

    + _____

e. _____

    − _____

    + _____

f. _____

    − _____

    + _____

g. _____

    − _____

    + _____

h. _____

    − _____

    + _____

i. _____
    – _____
    + _____

j. _____
    – _____
    + _____

k. _____
    – _____
    + _____

l. _____
    – _____
    + _____

m. _____
    – _____
    + _____

n. _____
    – _____
    + _____

o. _____
    – _____
    + _____

p. _____
    – _____
    + _____

q. _____
    – _____
    + _____

r. _____
    – _____
    + _____

s. _____

    − _____

    + _____

t. _____

    − _____

    + _____

u. _____

    − _____

    + _____

v. _____

    − _____

    + _____

w. _____

    − _____

    + _____

x. _____

    − _____

    + _____

y. _____

    − _____

    + _____

z. _____

    − _____

    + _____

List of personality traits that may contribute to MBS symptoms: Include traits such as perfectionism, low self-esteem, high expectations of self, worry, fear, anger, hostility, time urgency, guilt, dependency, isolation, needing to be good, needing to be liked, being overly conscientious, being hard on yourself, being overly responsible, harboring anger or resentment, and others. Try to think of anything and everything, and list each trait as a separate item. Include personality traits that were learned or developed in childhood as well as those you currently posess. While you're doing this exercise, put down anything that comes into your mind, even if you think it may have no connection to your MBS symptoms. **Ignore the lines with the minus and plus signs for now**.

a. _____

     − _____

     + _____

b. _____

     − _____

     + _____

c. _____

     − _____

     + _____

d. _____

     − _____

     + _____

e. _____

     − _____

     + _____

f. _____

     − _____

     + _____

g. _____

     − _____

     + _____

h. _____

     − _____

     + _____

i. _____

     − _____

     + _____

j. _____

    − _____

    + _____

k. _____

    − _____

    + _____

l. _____

    − _____

    + _____

m. _____

    − _____

    + _____

n. _____

    − _____

    + _____

o. _____

    − _____

    + _____

p. _____

    − _____

    + _____

q. _____

    − _____

    + _____

r. _____

    − _____

    + _____

s. _____

    − _____

    + _____

t. _____

    − _____

    + _____

u. _____

    − _____

    + _____

v. _____

    − _____

    + _____

w. _____

    − _____

    + _____

x. _____

    − _____

    + _____

y. _____

    − _____

    + _____

z. _____

    − _____

    + _____

Getting Started With the Write Away Process

Review the lists of current and past stressors and personality traits you have compiled. Without spending too much time deciding, list the two to three items in each of the areas that you think are most likely influencing your health. You will be writing on these issues this week. You can write on one issue for several days if necessary, or you can write on a different issue each day. Use your intuition to decide what issues are most important and to decide when you can move on to write about other issues.

Current Stressors

1.

2.

3.

Past Stressors

1.

2.

3.

Personality Traits

1.

2.

3.

You will be learning two techniques for the first week's assignments: clustering and free-writing.

Clustering, also referred to as "webbing," is an effective way to brainstorm your way to self-discovery. Clustering allows you to access ideas quickly, using the circling of your ideas on paper to help you more easily go between the right and left hemispheres of your brain, an ability that's key to solving problems (Rico, 1983).

The five steps to producing a cluster are:

1. Choose one topic/issue from one of your lists (past stressor, current stressor, or personality trait). Write it in the center of the oval (next page). This is the nucleus of your cluster.

2. Set a timer for five minutes.

3. Begin to "free associate" on the topic/issue. Open your mind and write down whatever thought occurs to you. Write it down in a one- to four-word phrase, and then circle what you've written and connect it by a line to the nucleus.

4. Now you have two possibilities to prompt your thinking: what you wrote in your nucleus or what you just wrote in the satellite circle and connected to it. Now write down a word or phrase that represents your next immediate idea, circle it, and connect it to the circle that prompted it.

5. Continue this process until the timer signals your five minutes is up. You will end up with a cluster of ideas and thoughts, which may look like a web filling the page.

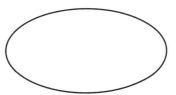

Free-writing—or "fast writing" as it more appropriately might be called—is a powerful technique that allows you to access important pieces of information and understand them better. It is a way to gain perspective, which may serve to free you from some of the issues that have caused you pain and suffering. The idea behind it is that when you write faster than you normally would, helpful material that you would usually censor before even writing it down is allowed to surface.

Natalie Goldberg (1986) refers to the outcome of free-writing as "first thoughts," and among her six-step process, includes:

1. Keep your hand moving. Write faster than you would normally write in a reflective mood; attempt instead to take dictation from your thoughts as they stream across the radar screen of your mind.

2. Don't cross out anything, even if you didn't mean to write what you did.

3. Don't worry about spelling, punctuation, or grammar.

4. Write whatever comes into your mind or comes from your hand.

5. Allow any thoughts and any feelings to be expressed.

On the following page, write the topic/issue from the nucleus of your cluster in the blank space of the sentence.

Set a timer for ten minutes. Do free-writing on whatever thoughts the sentence sparks until your time is up. When writing, allow yourself to express any emotions that you might have. Express things as strongly as you wish. Use phrases such as "I feel ____" and "I felt _____" often.

Many people learn things about themselves or others by doing this kind of writing. Often, what comes up is surprising.

My *feelings* about me and _____ include:

Complete this free-write by copying the following affirmation three times in the spaces below:

I am relieved to express these feelings.

-

-

-

Now fill in the blank in the sentence on the following page with the same item you put in your cluster nucleus and used in the first free-write.

Set your timer for another ten minutes. The idea in the next exercise is to process your feelings. Expressing emotions is important, but it is also critical to understand them, gain perspective on them, and begin to move past them. Therefore, in this free-write, make sure to use phrases such as "I see that...," "I realize...," "I hope that...," "I need to...," "I want to...," "I can...," "I will...," "I understand that...," "I appreciate...," "I wonder if...," "I have learned...," and "I have discovered..." Write whatever comes to your mind with a focus on understanding the topic/issue as best you can at this point in time. Of course, some feelings are likely to continue to be expressed, which is perfectly acceptable. Keep writing until your time is up.

My *understandings* about me and _____ include:

Complete this free-write by copying the following affirmation three times:

Understanding these issues helps me feel better.

-

-

-

You have just completed a 25-Minute Jog. It is common to feel relieved and in less pain after doing this writing exercise, but it is also not unusual to feel worse or have more pain. You are doing important work that deals with critical issues in your life, which have affected your mind and your body by causing MBS. Doing this work will free you from the symptoms of MBS, but it may not happen immediately. Sometimes people taking this program initially feel worse because they begin to stir up issues and emotions that were buried for a long time. They also might stir up conscious emotions or topics that they were unaware were affecting them so much. This is normal. Don't worry. In fact, if your symptoms either improve or worsen by doing the writing, that shows that these symptoms are truly caused by MBS. And when you see these symptoms change in any way (better, worse, moving from one spot to another, or shifting from one symptom to a different one), you are making progress!

Whatever you do, don't give up. Keep writing and keep doing this work. You will see changes within days or weeks.

For the rest of week one, do a 25-Minute Jog each day. You may decide to write about the same issue for several days or even all week, or you might decide you have finished with one issue and are ready to move to another one. You might find one issue too difficult to write on at first, and that's perfectly fine. You can approach it later as the program continues.

On the following pages, complete your 25-Minute Jogs for the first week. If you are unable to write on a certain day, don't worry. Do the best that you can. Remember not to be too hard on yourself. If you notice that you tend to be hard on yourself, you might want to do a 25-Minute Jog on that issue. Then you can practice being kind to yourself while you write.

Week One, Day Two:

Select a topic for today's free-write. Complete a five-minute cluster on this page. Then complete two ten-minute free-writes on the following pages.

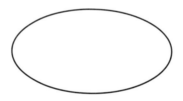

My *feelings* about me and _____ include:

Copy the following affirmation three times.

I am relieved to express these feelings.

-

-

-

My *understandings* about me and _____ include:

Copy the following affirmation three times.

Understanding these issues helps me feel better.

-

-

-

Week One, Day Three:

Select a topic for today's free-write. Complete a five-minute cluster for this page. Then complete two ten-minute free-writes on the following pages.

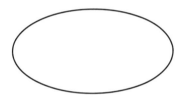

My *feelings* about me and _____ include:

Copy the following affirmation three times.

I am relieved to express these feelings.

-

-

-

My *understandings* about me and _____ include:

Copy the following affirmation three times.

Understanding these issues helps me feel better.

-

-

-

Week One, Day Four:

Select a topic for today's free-write. Complete a five-minute cluster for this page. Then complete two ten-minute free-writes on the following pages.

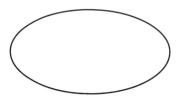

My *feelings* about me and _____ include:

Copy the following affirmation three times.

I am relieved to express these feelings.

-

-

-

My *understandings* about me and _____ include:

Copy the following affirmation three times.

Understanding these issues helps me feel better.

-

-

-

Week One, Day Five:

Select a topic for today's free-write. Complete a five-minute cluster for this page. Then complete two ten-minute free-writes on the following pages.

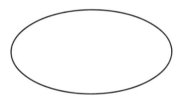

My *feelings* about me and _____ include:

Copy the following affirmation three times.

I am relieved to express these feelings.

-

-

-

My *understandings* about me and _____ include:

Copy the following affirmation three times.

Understanding these issues helps me feel better.

-

-

-

Week One, Day Six:

Select a topic for today's free-write. Complete a five-minute cluster for this page. Then complete two ten-minute free-writes on the following pages.

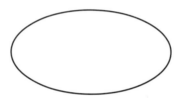

My *feelings* about me and _____ include:

Copy the following affirmation three times.

I am relieved to express these feelings.

-

-

-

My *understandings* about me and _____ include:

Copy the following affirmation three times.

Understanding these issues helps me feel better.

-

-

-

Week One, Day Seven:

Select a topic for today's free-write. Complete a five-minute cluster for this page. Then complete two ten-minute free-writes on the following pages.

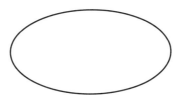

My *feelings* about me and _____ include:

Copy the following affirmation three times.

I am relieved to express these feelings.

-

-

-

My *understandings* about me and _____ include:

Copy the following affirmation three times.

Understanding these issues helps me feel better.

-

-

-

Reflections to Calm the Inner Mind

There are several reflective or meditative techniques that can be helpful in curing MBS and associated mind-body symptoms. You will learn them as you practice them. It is important to practice them in order to obtain the most benefit. The techniques you learn will last for your lifetime.

Meditation for Week One: Mindfulness Meditation

The first week's reflection is based upon the foundation of mindfulness meditation. I have been a mindfulness meditation teacher for fifteen years, and I have found it to be very helpful in learning to live life more fully, to appreciate what we have and who we are as a person, and to let go of things that have been or are bothering us. It is beyond the scope of this book to offer a comprehensive description of the philosophy and psychology of mindfulness meditation, which has existed for more than 2,500 years. Studies have shown that mindfulness can be effective in reducing pain and improving well-being (Kabat-Zinn, 1982; Grossman, et. al., 2007).

The basic concept of mindfulness is to learn to be focused, awake, and fully alive in the present moment. Mindfulness teaches us to face the present moment with interest and without judgment in order to be able to accept what has happened and learn that we cannot change what has happened. Once we accept the circumstances of the moment, we can make a good decision. We can decide to let go and move ahead to the next moment, to accept or to alter our reactions (thoughts and emotions) to what has occurred, or to act to change our situation. The philosophy of mindfulness teaches us that everything is transient and changing—our mood, our thoughts, our relationships, our family, our financial or work situation. It helps us understand that stress and pain are inevitable at different points in life. By practicing mindfulness, we learn that pain can be tolerated once we understand that we can control our response to it. For people with MBS, mindfulness can help to accept the past and to learn to choose our reactions to the present situation. Mindfulness teaches us to recognize and feel inner thoughts and emotions, to accept that they are there and that they will not harm us, and to let go of our reaction to them so that they don't continue to cause pain by keeping us locked into the stress and pain that emanates from our past.

Listen to the first track of the CD each day. If you have trouble falling asleep, listen to it at night and it will help you fall asleep. Many people listen to it early in the morning, and this often helps them set the tone for their day. You can also listen to it when you are in pain to help you relax, cope better with the pain, and realize that you can learn to alter your focus to areas of your body that are not in pain, thus helping you be more in control of your pain. You can download the meditation to an MP3 player and listen to it while you are walking or during a break at work. However, I don't recommend listening to the meditation while driving—sometimes people fall asleep to it!

Meditation Synopsis

Find a place where you won't be disturbed. Begin this exercise by paying attention to your breath. You don't need to breathe in any particular pattern or depth, just notice your breath with interest and curiosity. Try not to judge your breath at all, just notice it as if you were noticing a fine painting. After some time, you will likely notice that your mind has wandered away from the breath, and when that happens, notice that the mind wandered and gently turn your attention to the breath. The essence of this practice is being able to notice what is on your mind and choosing to pay attention to that without reacting to it, and then choosing to pay attention to something else—for example, noticing the next breath.

Then begin to slowly scan through the body. Notice each and every body part with the same interested, yet non-reacting mind. When you arrive at parts of the body that are uncomfortable, notice the discomfort with less judging or reacting, accepting that things are the way they are for now, then choosing to move on to the next part of the body, paying attention in the same way. Do this exercise with kindness to the body. After scanning each part of the body, say to yourself, "I fully and completely accept myself and my body."

Take some time to notice your thoughts and feelings. Do this in the same way: noticing without reacting, accepting each thought or feeling as "just a thought" or "just a feeling," and letting go of each in order to notice the next one. In this way, you will be developing the ability to not be controlled by thoughts or feelings, but to choose which ones you pay attention to and which ones you just let go of. This will be important in breaking some of the associations that have developed between your thoughts and feelings and your MBS symptoms.

When emotions arise, allow your mind to notice how these emotions are connected to past traumas, to current stressors, to your personality, or to reactions that occur in either the child-mind or the parent-mind. Notice these mental phenomena without having to react to them. Notice the connection, accept that is the way your mind works, and choose not to react to it, choose not to allow those mental images to affect you, and just simply let them go, just as you let each breath go. At the end of this exercise, repeat to yourself three times, "I fully and completely accept myself and my body."

Using Mindfulness During Your Day

You can also use these techniques throughout the day. Simply by taking a few moments to focus on your breathing, you can train yourself to let go of something that may be annoying, upsetting, or worrisome. If you pay close attention to the breath for a few moments, you are letting go of everything else. You may be able to teach yourself to notice your breath when pain occurs, as a way of turning attention away from the pain for a few moments.

When you can notice your thoughts with the awareness that they are "just thoughts" and that you don't have to be bothered by them, you don't have to act on them, and that you can just choose to let them go, you are taking a tremendous step towards freeing yourself from some of the chains that have imprisoned you into MBS. When you can do the same thing with emotions, such as fear, anger, guilt, shame, or worry, then you are closer to freeing yourself from the grip of pain that has been created by keeping these emotions inside of you.

From mindfulness practice, you learn that your body is strong and healthy. You can pay attention to all aspects of your body, not just the areas that hurt, and view your whole body as being well. The pain you experience due to MBS is transient. It will go away. You are learning to control it because you know what causes it, and you are learning techniques to overcome it. Listen to this meditation, and practice living mindfully. It will not only help to free yourself from MBS, it will teach you to appreciate your life on a deep level.

Reprogramming the Brain

As you are now aware, your brain has developed pathways that are causing your MBS symptoms. These pathways are real and have developed because of the stressful events in your life, the (often subconscious) emotions that were generated by these events, and the internal stress that you put on yourself. These pathways that have created pain and other symptoms are learned and can be un-learned. This section introduces you to one of the most important and useful components of the program.

For you to cure MBS, the nerve pathways that continue to produce pain or other MBS symptoms need to be interrupted. There are two basic ways to accomplish this. You can undo these pathways or learn new pathways to take their place. Research studies show that when you change how you think or how you react to stressful situations, you are actually changing your brain and its pathways (Doidge, 2007; Begley, 2008). The brain can actually grow new nerve cells and develop new pathways over time. Exercises that reprogram the mind teach you to activate the conscious part of the brain to override the subconscious pathways that produce and maintain pain and MBS. When you practice these exercises, you are changing your brain. The more you practice, the quicker you will get better. Studies of people who have had strokes show that they can rewire their brains (Taub, 2006). With enough practice, they relearn how to use their limbs that were paralyzed. This usually takes a great deal of time and practice. Fortunately, reprogramming pain patterns often takes much less time; however, everyone is different, so don't worry if you don't see changes immediately. It may be necessary to repeat the following exercises for several weeks until your brain responds with new pain-free pathways.

Reprogramming MBS Symptoms: Week One Exercises

The following exercises give you methods of talking to your mind and your body. This self-talk will help you to override the pain pathways. It may seem silly to talk to yourself, but it really works. You are going to take charge of your pain; you're going to overcome it by force of will power. I don't advise ignoring your MBS symptoms and hoping that they will go away. Ignoring symptoms can be similar to ignoring the puppy who is chewing the furniture, he will just keep doing it until he is taught that it is unacceptable. You may find it takes many repetitions for your mind to stop producing the pain pathways. Keep it up as if you are training a puppy.

EXERCISE 1:

When pain or other symptoms occur, stop and take a deep breath. Then take a moment

to remind yourself that there is nothing seriously wrong with your body. You are healthy, and the MBS symptoms will subside soon. Tell your mind that you realize that the symptoms are just a way of warning you about underlying feelings of fear, guilt, anger, anxiety, shame, inadequacy, or other emotions. Tell your mind to stop producing the symptoms immediately. Do this with force and conviction, either out loud or silently. Take a few deep breaths, and move on with what you were doing.

This is the basic exercise to help you take control of your symptoms. It's an affirmation of your health that works because it activates the DLPFC, the conscious part of the brain that reduces pain. It is critical that you believe in the importance of this exercise and that you believe fully in your ability to improve your symptoms by altering your mind. At first, you may feel embarrassed or self-conscious to talk to yourself, but I've found these affirmations to be amazingly successful for defeating MBS. So, believe in them. Do them with enthusiasm! If you are so inclined, I even give you permission to curse. In fact, a recent research study showed that using swear words is helpful in reducing pain (Stephens, 2009).

Many people are faced with constant pain, and they could spend their whole day talking to their mind and their body. In this situation, you will need to practice this exercise very frequently, but certainly not all day. Even if you don't see results initially, keep practicing—it may take some time to retrain the brain.

Reprogramming Thoughts and Emotions Connected to MBS Symptoms

It is critical to begin to notice thoughts and emotions as they occur. Everyone has a large number of them during the day. Most go unnoticed and can add to the buildup of emotions in the subconscious. One day I was walking into the kitchen, and I suddenly noticed a sharp pain that occurred in four spots in my back simultaneously. The pain lasted a few minutes and seemed to come from "out of the blue." I immediately stopped what I was doing and tried to notice what was going on in my mind. I asked myself, "What were you thinking about?" My first reaction was that I wasn't thinking about anything. So I asked again. This time it came to me. I'd been thinking about a conflict I was having with a relative.

Thoughts and emotions are constantly bubbling below the surface of our consciousness. You can't notice every one of them, but the more you train yourself to notice mental events, the better you will be at connecting your thoughts and emotions to MBS symptoms. Once you begin to make these connections, you are well on your way to getting better.

During your day, try to identify any emotions such as fear, anger, resentment, guilt, hurt, or shame that occur, whether they happen when you are having MBS symptoms or at other times. **It is important to recognize that all of your thoughts and emotions are normal.** Everyone has thoughts and emotions that appear to be at times silly, weird, dangerous, petty, fearful, and even evil. You can learn to notice a wide variety of thoughts and emotions yet stop your mind and body from reacting to them with pain or other MBS symptoms.

One way to categorize these emotions is to consider them as coming from the inner child-mind (for example, "I am mad," "I want more," "I feel afraid") or from the inner parent-mind (for example, "You should know better," "You should do more," "You are no good"). Sometimes you'll find that both of these types of emotions occur almost at the same time or that one type triggers the other. When you notice any of these emotions, do the next exercise to reprogram your mind to reduce the symptoms they may be causing.

EXERCISE 2:

When you notice emotions during the day, whether they are associated with any symptoms or not, stop and take a deep breath. Then take a moment to talk to your mind. Tell yourself that your emotions and feelings are normal. Accept that you have these thoughts and that they may be very strong at times. Take another deep breath to allow the feelings to settle. Pay attention to what is causing the emotion.

Then tell yourself that you won't allow these thoughts and emotions to continue to cause MBS symptoms any longer. Do this firmly and assertively. Tell your mind that you are going to learn to have feelings without having the reactions that cause MBS. Tell your mind that you are going to deal with the things causing the emotions, so your mind doesn't need to warn you of a problem. It can just relax and allow the MBS symptoms to disappear. Take another deep breath and move on.

Some people find it helpful to categorize feelings by determining if the emotion is coming from the inner child-mind or the inner parent-mind. If the emotion is generated by the child-mind, treat it as you would treat a child: tell it to calm down, that you realize it is upset or angry, that this is a normal reaction to current events that are triggered by earlier life experiences, and allow it to just relax and let those feelings go. If this doesn't work, stop and assertively tell the child-mind to stop it immediately. Remind the inner child that you are the boss—you are in control, and you won't allow fears or resentment to dominate your life anymore.

If the emotion is generated by the parent-mind, treat your mind as you would an intrusive parent, by telling the parent-mind to relax and leave you alone, that you know what the parent-mind is saying and you realize these thoughts and emotions are there because of earlier stressful experiences. However, you can choose to respond to this inner parent by listening but ignoring any unwanted and unhelpful advice. If the emotion or inner voice is very strong, you may need to forcefully tell the inner parent to stop immediately and be quiet. Remind the inner parent voice that this is your life and you can let go of guilt and self-criticism in order to live as you please.

Reprogramming Triggers to MBS Symptoms

As described in chapter 3, many people find that their pain or other MBS symptoms are triggered by certain situations or activities. For example, you may find that sitting, bending in a certain way, eating certain foods, or interacting with certain people may trigger the onset of symptoms. You may try to avoid these triggers to avoid having pain. It is generally not a good idea to avoid coming into contact with your triggers. The more you avoid them, the greater power they begin to have over you. Avoiding certain foods or locations or positions or activities can create fear and insecurity. Fear and insecurity will create more pain. It is much better to meet your triggers head on and learn to overcome them. The more you practice doing this, the sooner you will improve.

Complete the list provided here to help you become aware of these triggers and alert you to any associations that have developed over time.

List of triggers that may precipitate symptoms: Make a list of the activities, movements, thoughts, emotions, times, places, etc. that are associated with your symptoms. Include anything that occurs at the same time or just before the symptoms occur.

List any activities, movements, places, positions, thoughts, emotions, people, situations, foods, weather changes, or anything else that triggers your symptoms.

a. _____

b. _____

c. _____

d. _____

e. _____

f. _____

g. _____

h. _____

i. _____

j. _____

k. _____

l. _____

m. _____

n. _____

o. _____

p. _____

q. _____

r. _____

s. _____

When you are about to encounter or you are encountering any of these triggers, either before or after you have developed any symptoms, follow the guidelines given below to prevent the symptoms from occurring or to reduce them.

EXERCISE 3:

When you notice you are encountering any triggers to the symptoms or any stressful situations, immediately stop and take a deep breath. Then take a moment to remind your mind that this activity or trigger will NOT cause any symptoms or problems any more. For example, when I lift heavy items I always remind myself, "This will not cause any back problems. My back is healthy and strong, and I can do this without pain." It is important to have a deep understanding of MBS and the fact that your body is healthy and that you can get better by using these methods.

Keep reminding yourself that you will not be allowing your mind to produce MBS symptoms this time. Be firm and assertive. Repeat whatever positive phrases you choose every time you encounter any of your triggers until your brain unlearns MBS pathways.

The more you encounter your triggers, the more opportunity you will have to overcome them and return to health. You can choose to take on your triggers, either gradually or more rapidly. You might choose to start exercising, driving more often, eating foods you've avoided, or going out in certain weather. Challenge yourself, and push forward to reprogram your brain.

EXERCISE 4:

Finally, it is important to take a few moments each day to stop and take a deep breath and remind yourself that your body is physically fine—you do not have a serious illness. Remind your subconscious mind that you are aware of the cause of the symptoms and that you will not allow stressful events and emotions to cause these symptoms any more. Take a few more deep breaths, and move on with your day.

These are all of the exercises and assignments for the first week of the program. Doing all of these activities will take approximately an hour or even more each day. That is a large commitment, and it is important to do the best you can. It is also important to realize that you have other important things in your life and that you will probably not be able to complete every exercise this week. As I've mentioned before, the most important thing to do while you take this program is to be kind to yourself. Remember that you are doing this for yourself and that you need to take time for yourself in order to get better. You deserve that time, and you deserve to live your life without pain or other MBS symptoms.

chapter 8

Week Two: Reclaiming the Past

May I have the courage today
To live the life I would love,
To postpone my dream no longer,
But do at last what I came here for
And waste my heart on fear no more.
— John O'Donohue

It matters not how strait the gate,
How charged with punishments the scroll.
I am the master of my fate:
I am the captain of my soul.
— William Ernest Henley

Once you start doing this work, MBS symptoms often change. Sometimes, they start to get better and then get worse, or get worse for a short time before they get better. MBS symptoms can move from one part of the body to another or shift from one symptom, such as pain, to another one, such as fatigue, anxiety, or dizziness. These changes are all signs that you are able to alter the symptoms by doing psychological work, and confirm that you are on the right track. Remember that you will be successful if you keep doing this work. The exercises in this program are relatively simple, but they are not always easy. It is hard work to face your stressors and to face your own mind and body, which has been perpetuating your symptoms. But it is the work you must do to rid yourself of these symptoms and to improve your life.

If you look closely and are honest with yourself, you will most likely be able to find several issues or events from your childhood or adolescence that were stressful to you and that have set up the amygdala, the ACC, and the ANS to react to later stresses with MBS symptoms. In the exercises for this week, we are going to focus on some of the issues from your past and help you to cope with them better and see them in a different light.

Revising the Past Exercise

This exercise is based upon recent scientific evidence about memory and the role that emotional memories can play in our lives. Scientists who study memory have learned that our memories are not only often inaccurate, but they are constantly changing (Roemer, et. al., 1998; Schafe, et. al., 2001). This is surprising to most people. When I was young, my brother burned his leg badly and tried to hide it from our parents. I vividly recall seeing him in pain, discovering the burn, and running to get help. The problem with this memory is that it didn't happen that way at all. All of our other family members recall that I had nothing to do with discovering the burn or getting help. How could I have such a vivid memory of an event (my role in getting help) that never happened?

It turns out that this is an extremely common occurrence. This is why eyewitness accounts of crimes or identification of suspects is often inaccurate. Ten months after a catastrophic airplane crash in the Netherlands, a study found that 55 percent of people reported actually seeing the airplane crash, although no video of the crash existed (Crombag, et. al., 1996). Studies have shown that memories of events shift and alter over time in most people. We remember certain aspects of events or forget other aspects of events as we get older.

Conventional wisdom suggests that we learn to accept that the past is behind us and that we can't change it, and therefore we should try to accept it as it is in order to move forward. This appears to make a lot of sense. However, since your past is merely a summation of your memory of it, and your memory is constantly changing, your past is actually also changing all the time.

Some people who have had traumatic events in their life and continue to have reactions to these events are considered to have post-traumatic stress disorder (PTSD). People with PTSD have outpourings of activity from the autonomic nervous system, which leads to fear and anxiety whenever they recall the traumatic events that triggered the disorder. About a fifth of all combat veterans develop some form of PTSD (Beckham, et. al., 1997). As discussed in chapter 3, there is a very large overlap between PTSD and Mind Body Syndrome. This makes sense, because both PTSD and MBS are triggered by the same kinds of stressful or traumatic events. Furthermore, the brain pathways and structures that activate and perpetuate the symptoms of MBS and PTSD are the same. I consider

MBS to be a form of PTSD in which the symptoms tend to be manifest in the body (often with pain), rather than with anxiety.

People with PTSD who are successfully treated are those who learn to adapt to their prior traumatic events. One way of accomplishing this is by learning to view and experience their memories differently. They develop ways to make these difficult memories less problematic and easier to accept and cope with. Since our memories are constantly changing and since these memories can affect MBS as well as PTSD symptoms, why not actively work to change our past in ways that allow us to heal and let go of stressful memories? This is precisely what this week's exercises are designed to accomplish.

Review the three lists that you completed in chapter 7: past stressors or traumatic events, current stressors, and personality traits (see pages 72, 75 and 78). Some of these items may produce extremely negative emotions, as many people have been exposed to horrific events. Despite these difficulties, it is important to be able to move on and place these events in perspective. One way of doing this is to learn to change our view of these events to some degree.

Between each of the items you have placed on these lists, there is a line with a "-" and a "+" on it. The "-" line is there to remind you of the negative aspects of these events or traits, but do not complete that line. On the "+" line, write something that is a positive that occurred due to that negative experience or trait. This may be difficult for many people, but it can help you to let go of the grip of the past.

Look to find something positive, even if it might be a very small positive, about each stressor from the past and the present and each personality trait. You might write: "It helped me to understand myself" or "It allowed me to be compassionate to others in a similar situation." Maybe some positive things occurred due to the event—for example, you learned that you could survive or take care of yourself or that you could trust some people but not others. See if you can look carefully at what you have learned from your past experiences and find some ways in which you've benefited from even the most difficult experiences.

It is important to recognize that the past is simply our memory of it. Finding something positive in these events helps to ease some of the hurt and change how you view these stressors, which in turn helps you to let go and move on. When you do that, it will also help you to learn to find positives in your current stressors so that they can become more manageable. Finally, this exercise will help you gain perspective on some of your personality traits that can affect MBS.

Writing Exercise for Week Two: Unsent Letters

As you are now well aware, one of the causes of MBS is holding emotions inside. We often are unable to express some of these emotions verbally for a variety of reasons. The person we need to talk to may be gone from our lives, unavailable, or simply impossible to talk to. There are some things that one simply can't express to a boss, neighbor, or relative. Many emotions stem from many years ago, and the person involved may have changed. Yet we still may be hanging on to feelings that have been bothering us for years or decades. One way to express these feelings in a safe and useful way is to write letters that we do not send (Rainer, 1978).

Unsent letters are useful to express negative feelings that we have been harboring and that are causing us harm, such as unexpressed anger, resentment, fear, guilt, or shame. However, it is also important to express gratitude and thankfulness to those whom we may have not had a chance to thank. Sometimes, we need to write letters of love, apology, or regret to those who are now missing from our lives.

Create a list of possible recipients to whom you might send an unsent letter. These letters will allow you to explore whatever you need to explore regarding your relationships. You may need to write to a parent, relative, current or former spouse, significant other, child, friend, neighbor, colleague, boss, or coworker. You may need to write to someone who has died or a person from whom you are estranged, as well as to people who are present in your life today. You can write to groups of people or to a president, a Pope, or God. It can also be very helpful to write to yourself, to your pain, to your subconscious mind, or to yourself when you were a child.

My list of possible "recipients" of an unsent letter includes:

_____

_____

_____

_____

_____

_____

_____

_____

_____

_____

_____

_____

_____

_____

_____

_____

_____

_____

_____

_____

_____

_____

_____

_____

_____

Each day, you will be choosing one of the recipients listed to write an unsent letter to. Take a look at your list now, and circle the people that you think it might be most helpful for you to write to first. Once you begin writing, you may discover you need to send several letters to the same person. Feel free to do this if necessary. Then you may choose to move on to other letters.

When you write, feel free to allow your mind and hand to write whatever needs to be said to the person or entity you've chosen to address. Since the letter will not be sent, you can say anything that comes to your mind without censoring it. You might choose to use profanity, for example, or to express extreme emotion. This is perfectly acceptable and can help to relieve tension in the subconscious mind.

Trust that you are safe in writing this letter and that you can express any thoughts or feelings that cross your mind. Write as long as you need to, but typically ten to fifteen minutes is reasonable. Use additional pages if you need more space. When you start writing, you may be surprised by the strength of the emotions you have been holding in.

After each letter, reflect on and write a description of what you have learned from this person, what you have gained from your interaction with this person (even if the interaction was very destructive), and in what ways you may have grown as a result of your relationship with this person. State how you've been able to deal with any issues related to this relationship and how you plan on dealing with any unresolved issues. Write these reflections in a letter to yourself. See Rainer (1978) for more information on this type of writing.

Week Two, Day One:

Date and write a letter below to a person or entity from your unsent letter list. Express your thoughts and feelings fully. Use as much paper as needed. Remember to sign your name.

Dear _____,

Now write the following affirmation three times—fill in the name of the person to whom you addressed the letter:

It is helpful to explore my relationship with _____.

-
-
-

Write a letter to yourself reflecting on the unsent letter you just finished. What have you learned from this person or your interaction? What have you learned from writing this letter? How have you dealt with any issues related to this relationship? How do you plan on dealing with these issues in the future?

Dear _____,

Week Two, Day Two:

Choose a recipient for today's unsent letter.

Dear _____,

Now write the following affirmation three times—fill in the name of the person to whom you addressed the letter:

It is helpful to explore my relationship with _____.

-

-

-

Write a letter to yourself to reflect upon the letter you just wrote.

Dear _____,

Week Two, Day Three:

Choose a recipient for today's unsent letter.

Dear _____,

Now write the following affirmation three times—fill in the name of the person to whom you addressed the letter:

It is helpful to explore my relationship with _____.

-

-

-

Write a letter to yourself to reflect upon the letter you just wrote.

Dear _____,

Week Two, Day Four:

Choose a recipient for today's unsent letter.

Dear _____,

Now write the following affirmation three times—fill in the name of the person to whom you addressed the letter:

It is helpful to explore my relationship with _____.

-

-

-

Write a letter to yourself to reflect upon the letter you just wrote.

Dear _____,

Week Two, Day Five:

Choose a recipient for today's unsent letter.

Dear _____,

Now write the following affirmation three times—fill in the name of the person to whom you addressed the letter:

It is helpful to explore my relationship with _____.

-

-

-

Write a letter to yourself to reflect upon the letter you just wrote.

Dear _____,

Week Two, Day Six:

Choose a recipient for today's unsent letter.

Dear _____,

Now write the following affirmation three times—fill in the name of the person to whom you addressed the letter:

It is helpful to explore my relationship with _____.

-

-

-

Write a letter to yourself to reflect upon the letter you just wrote.

Dear _____,

Week Two, Day Seven:

Choose a recipient for today's unsent letter.

Dear _____,

Now write the following affirmation three times—fill in the name of the person to whom you addressed the letter:

It is helpful to explore my relationship with _____.

-

-

-

Write a letter to yourself to reflect upon the letter you just wrote.

Dear _____,

Meditation for Week Two: Revising the Past Through Mindfulness Techniques

You will find the reflection or meditation for this week on the second track of the CD. Listen to this track every day this week, if you are able. Continue to listen to and practice the techniques from the first track as well. You might choose to listen to one track in the morning and the other at lunchtime or in the evening. The meditations are designed to teach you techniques to calm both the conscious and the subconscious mind, to reduce activity of the autonomic nervous system, and to create some time for yourself.

This meditation will help you cope better with some of the issues in your life by asking you to review them and consider them in a new light. It builds upon and uses the lists of positives that you completed with regard to the past stressors, current stressors, and personality traits. Each time you listen to this track, you are asked to consider some of these stressors or traits and think about them without developing as many negative reactions. The more you are able to decrease negative emotions about these issues, the easier it will be to let go of them and free yourself from their hold over you and your body. The following paragraphs give a description of the meditation.

Meditation Synopsis

Find a spot where you will not be disturbed for several minutes. Start with the basic breathing technique of noticing each breath, accepting it as it is, and letting each breath go. Mentally, begin to review some of your past experiences. Realize that you are in control. You will be able to notice these experiences without reacting to them as you may have done in the past, just as you notice each breath.

Begin with some of the items on your list of current stressors, prior traumatic experiences, and personality issues. For each traumatic experience, notice how the mind has reacted to this in the past—how the child-mind of the subconscious may have gotten angry, resentful, afraid, hurt, or ashamed; or how the parent-mind of the subconscious may have tried to shame you, "should" you, or belittle you. Recognize that these are perfectly normal reactions of the mind. When you notice how the subconscious has given you these messages, instruct the subconscious mind to "calm down," to stop reacting this way, to let the issue go. On occasion, you may need to instruct the subconscious more forcefully, as you might a demanding child or an intrusive parent. Recognize that past experiences are over, that you don't need to let them affect you any more, and that you have learned something from them. Even though some of these experiences may have been very difficult (or even horrible), there have been some positive things that have come from each one.

For each current stressor, recognize that it is real and that your subconscious mind reacts to it with the child-mind and the parent-mind. Remind yourself that you will learn something from each issue and that it need not cause any physical symptoms. You can instruct the child-mind to "relax" and "get over it." You can instruct the parent-mind to stop blaming or criticizing. Finally, find something positive in each current stressor to notice.

For each personality issue, recognize that these traits—such as guilt, self-criticism, being overly responsible, perfectionism—do exist and have been part of you for a long time. Recognize that there are some positive aspects of these traits. Remind yourself that you don't have to react with anger, guilt, fear, or shame to these personality traits. Instruct your mind not to allow any of these personality traits to cause any physical symptoms.

Do this each day with two to three items on your list until you have covered most of them. As you do this, many of the underlying emotions that have built up in the subconscious will gradually diminish. Also, notice that the body is healing as the mind is developing new paths to health and well-being. Notice some of the positive things you have in your life, such as pride in doing these exercises, self-esteem in being able to develop new ways of being, appreciation of those around you who care about you, and value in being alive.

Repeat these sentences three times: "I fully and completely accept myself. I let go of issues that have bothered me in the past. I choose to respond to my current stressors so they don't affect my health. I realize that I am not perfect, but I choose to accept my personality as it is, and I will not let any of these issues affect my health. I take pride in doing this work, which helps me to be in control and more healthy in mind and body."

Reprogramming the Brain: Week Two Exercises

The exercises for this week to reprogram the brain combine some affirmations with a couple of acupuncture points. These points are intended to calm the mind, and pressing on them sends new signals to the brain which will help to alter your brain's response to the old painful or emotion-producing signals.

As you do these exercises, continue to do the reprogramming the brain exercises from week one. For this week's exercises, there are two acupuncture points to learn. They are located on your hands, and you can press on them while you are in the midst of situations that may be stressful. Both of these points were chosen because they are easy to locate and use during the day.

Houxi (pronounced "Ho-shee") is located on the side of the palm. You can find it by looking at the palm of your hand and following the long palm crease that is closest to your fingers towards the pinkie side of your palm. This crease will end right on the side of the hand (see picture). Press deeply at this spot while repeating the phrases suggested below.

The other acupuncture point you can use is known as Hegu or Hoku. This point is located on the back of the hand in the fleshy area between the thumb and the first finger (see picture). If you press deeply in this area, you will feel a tender spot. You can press on this point while saying the reprogramming exercises found below. Use whichever point you prefer.

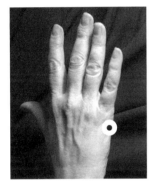 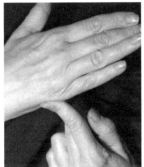 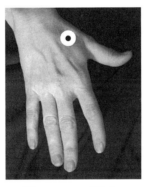 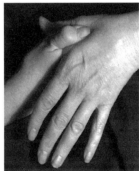

Houxi   *Hegu or Hoku*

1. When any of your MBS symptoms occur, stop and take a deep breath. Then rub one of the acupuncture points (either Houxi or Hegu on either hand) and say the following to yourself or out loud if you are able:

"Even though I am feeling _____ (fill in the symptom), I fully and completely accept myself. I know these sensations are caused by MBS and that I am healthy. I will not allow this symptom to continue or to bother me. I am going to recover fully." Repeat this three times while continuing to rub the acupuncture point.

2. When you notice emotions, whether they are associated with any symptoms or not, use this exercise. It is important to notice emotions as they occur during your day. The more you notice when you are upset, afraid, resentful, or feel guilty, the better you will be at recognizing and dealing with emotions in order to prevent them from perpetuating MBS symptoms.

When you notice any feelings, stop and take a deep breath. Then rub an acupuncture point while saying the following:

"Even though I am feeling _____ (fill in the emotion), I fully and completely accept myself. I know these emotions are normal reactions. I will not allow this emotion to cause MBS symptoms or stop my recovery." Repeat this three times while continuing to rub the acupuncture point.

3. When you notice you are encountering triggers to your MBS symptoms or any stressful situations, immediately stop and take a deep breath. Then rub an acupuncture point while saying the following:

"Even though I am encountering this situation _____ (fill in the trigger), I fully and completely accept myself. This situation is normal and does not need to cause MBS symptoms anymore. I will not allow this situation to cause a symptom or stop my recovery." Repeat this three times while continuing to rub the acupuncture point.

4. Finally, it is important to take a few moments each day to stop and take a deep breath, rub an acupuncture point, and remind yourself that your body is physically fine, that you do not have a serious illness. Repeat the following:

"I do not have a serious physical or emotional illness. I am healthy and am overcoming MBS. I fully and completely accept myself, and I am proud that I am doing this work."

By doing these exercises, you will gradually but completely reprogram your brain to stop producing pain, discomfort, or any other symptoms. Remember to take several moments each day, the more the better, to perform these reprogramming exercises. Don't get discouraged if the results are not immediate. It may have taken many years for these patterns to develop, and it may take some time for them to fade away.

Rebuilding Your Life

In order to advance beyond the ruts that we tend to get stuck in, it may be necessary to rebuild some aspects of our lives. Sometimes people with chronic pain or other symptoms lose the ability to function in their usual ways or feel stuck in their lives. Consider these thoughts as you complete the exercises for this week.

1. Decide that you can be pain free (or symptom free).

It is possible for you to get better. Develop and maintain this attitude, and remind yourself of this daily. Since there is nothing permanently wrong with your body, you will be able to feel better as you work through this program. It may take some time, but do not give up hope. If you keep working on this program, you will understand yourself better and understand the relationship between the mind and the body. These understandings, along with practicing the exercises, will help you get better.

2. Figure out what you want to do.

Given that you are going to get better, you can consider your next steps. It is critical to have a purpose in life. Begin to ask yourself questions such as: What are my skills? What things do I really like to do? What work would bring me pleasure and be meaningful? How can I make my current job more meaningful and pleasurable? What leisure activities are meaningful and bring me pleasure? How can I contribute to the world, to my community, to the people around me, to my family? What things do I need to leave behind or let go of? What parts of myself do I need to let go of, and what parts of myself do I want to nourish or emphasize?

3. Look at the big picture.

Take some time each day to think about life in general. Consider your gifts, what you have been given by others, and the material things you have. Be grateful for what you have. Consider the role of religion or spirituality in your life. Ask yourself what is important to you and what you should do each day to improve your life and the lives of others around you.

4. Possibility

Consider any and all possibilities for yourself. Picture a future that includes a healthier and a more productive you. Begin to include elements of that "new you" into your day, every day. When you wake up in the morning, envision some of these possibilities and carry them with you throughout the whole day.

5. Kindness to self

One of the most important aspects of ridding yourself of MBS and improving your psychological health is be kind to yourself. I cannot emphasize this enough. It is very easy to develop and maintain a self-critical attitude that can block recovery from MBS. I urge you to take time each day to be kind to yourself. You can do this by listening to meditations, by doing the writing exercises, by catching yourself in self-critical thoughts, and by doing some things for yourself. This is a simple yet powerful aspect of this program.

If you miss doing some of the homework, be kind to yourself. If you forget a task or don't finish all the work or errands on your list, be kind to yourself. Here are some examples of what I mean by being kind to yourself:

- Accepting that you are human and that you cannot be everything to everyone.
- Accepting your faults and realizing that you are a good person.
- Forgiving yourself for your mistakes, just as you would forgive others whom you love.
- Learning to say "no" to certain requests
- Taking time for yourself.
- Realizing that you are an important person on this earth and that you deserve to be happy and healthy.

.

You don't need to suffer for things that have happened in the past. You can change your life and improve your health by learning this simple yet powerful message.

6. Develop a plan of action for the week.

What activities can you do this week that will further your recovery? Decide that you are going to do physical activities that are good for you, such as walking or exercising. Plan to do some mental activities that are good for you, such as reading a book, doing crossword puzzles, or playing cards or board games. Make sure that you do something pleasurable for yourself each week, such as seeing a movie, taking a hot bath, or getting a massage. Agree to see other people in comfortable surroundings, such as going to church or getting together with friends for coffee, a meal, or for a walk.

Most people with MBS tend to think more about others and do more things for others than they do for themselves. If you are one of these people, it is critical that you begin to take some time for yourself each week. Arrange your schedule to do this. Ask those around you to help you find this time. Do not let this time be taken away from you. Find activities that will be enjoyable and fun, and make sure that you do them without feeling any guilt about taking time for yourself. You need this time for your healing process.

When you consider which activites to do, think about the triggers which have become connected to your pain or other MBS symptoms. As you will recall, triggers are learned responses in your brain and need to be overcome for complete healing. The more you encounter these triggers and reprogram your brain to overcome them, the quicker you will get better. When you continually avoid the triggers, you give them more power over you. Plan to overcome some triggers this week.

On the following list, write down some things that you might like to do in the next week, the next month, and in the next six months to one year. Feel free to put down anything that appeals to you. You are not making a commitment to do any of these right now; you are brainstorming about ideas that would improve your life or give you happiness.

Exercise: Things I Would Like to Do

Activities that will be productive and/or overcome triggers:

This week:

In the next month:

In the next six months to one year:

Things that are just for me:

This week:

In the next month:

In the next six months to one year:

Things I can do for others that would give me pleasure:

This week:

In the next month:

In the next six months to one year:

During this week, pick out one or two things from each of the above categories and see if you can do them. Plan ahead, and make sure you can accomplish them. You are doing them for yourself, and you deserve to do them. You deserve to be happier and to be free of MBS symptoms. And it is important to realize that as you become happier in your life and more comfortable with yourself, you will be taking big steps towards unlearning your pain.

chapter 9

Week Three: Dialogues Towards Understanding

Our own life is the instrument with which we experiment with truth.
— Thich Nat Hanh

In the last two weeks of the program, there will be a bit of a shift in tone—a bigger emphasis on the present and the future, rather than on the past. There will be more of an emphasis on the positives and on rebuilding your life. There is also an emphasis on allowing your body and mind to work together in harmony towards health. Hopefully, you are beginning to understand much more about yourself and some of the triggers in your past and present that have caused or exacerbated your MBS symptoms. Recognizing some of these issues can be uncomfortable or can create tension or pain in your life, but it is critically important for you to learn to resolve them, cope with them, express your feelings about them, move on to forgive others and yourself, and let go. By doing this important work, you will be taking the necessary steps towards healing. When you are able to make these strides towards achieving peace of mind, your body will be only too happy to let go of the pain and other symptoms that it has produced.

This program asks you to do a tremendous amount of work. And this work can be time-consuming and difficult because of the emotions that may get activated. The people who improve with this program are those who are courageous enough to tackle these exercises. The people who succeed are usually those who are persistent even or especially in the face of emotional issues that arise. In fact, many people improve only after they actually take actions to confront or deal with specific issues that are troubling them.

I also want to warn you about a common problem that may arise while working on this program. As I have pointed out earlier, many people with MBS are exceptionally hardworking and perfectionistic. They often put a lot of pressure on themselves and have high expectations for themselves. They may tend to criticize themselves. If they are unable to do every bit of homework in this program, they often begin to get down on themselves, which only makes matters worse. They may believe that they won't get better unless they complete every assignment. Do not fall into this trap. Few people complete each and every assignment, yet most people get better. Do as much as you can within the constraints of your daily life.

Writing Exercise for Week Three: Dialogues

There are two types of writing exercises for you to begin this week. The first one consists of dialogues. A dialogue is basically a conversation that you create in a written form. In a dialogue, you have the opportunity to express yourself to someone (or some entity), and to hear some things that you may need to hear from the other person or entity. One reason for writing these dialogues is to gain insight and learn more about important issues in your life. Dialogues may help you better understand situations that are confusing to you or those about which you need to make important decisions. Some of the dialogues may be short, ten-minute jottings, while others may be longer pieces that you return to again and again to explore whatever you need to explore regarding a relationship you have with a part of yourself or another.

The first step is to make a list of possible dialogues you might create. You may need to dialogue with a parent, another relative, a current or former spouse, significant other, friend, neighbor, colleague, boss, or coworker. You may choose to dialogue with someone who has died or a person from whom you are estranged, as well as with people who are present in your life today. You can dialogue with people whom you've never met, with religious leaders, political figures, or even God. Some of these may be recipients of unsent letters, but there are other entities that you might want to consider dialoguing with. For example, you may want to "converse" with one or more body parts that are causing you discomfort. You could dialogue with parts of your subconscious mind, such as the internal parent (who may push you to do all the things you "should" do) or the internal child (who may become angry or afraid). You may choose to dialogue with an event or situation in its entirety, not just a person involved in it. You can even dialogue with a business or an institution. Use your imagination, and be creative. If there is someone or something that is causing you stress in your life, you can write an imaginary dialogue and see what you can learn in order to help ease your mind or figure out how to better deal with it.

Consider all of these factors and any of the exercises you've done so far in this program and create a list of possible people or entities that you would like to engage in dialogue. Use the space provided to compile a list. Most dialogues will be between you and another person or entity.

My list of possible dialogues includes:

_____

_____

_____

_____

_____

_____

_____

_____

_____

_____

_____

_____

_____

_____

_____

_____

_____

_____

_____

Select Those Dialogues You Think Might Prove Most Beneficial

During this week, you will be choosing a person or entity each day for a dialogue. Take a look at your list now, and circle the ones that you think it might be most helpful for you to write first. Once you begin writing, you may discover you need to continue a dialogue for more than one day with the same person or thing. Feel free to do this as necessary. Once you see what you need to learn or express, you can move on to dialogue with other people or entities.

Some people have found it helpful to dialogue with a group (as if creating a meeting or conference call). For example, you could dialogue with yourself, your pain, and your subconscious mind.

Getting a Dialogue Started

When you write, feel free to allow your mind and hand to write whatever needs to be said to the person, situation, or entity you've chosen to address. Since the dialogue will remain on paper, you can say anything that comes to your mind without censoring what you write.

A good way to begin a dialogue is by writing a simple statement or a question. See what response might arise. Let your mind, your heart, and your hand go in whatever direction they will. Allow the person, situation, or entity to respond with whatever comes into your mind about how they might respond. It is important to be able to listen to what arises. Many people have found that they need to learn something from others in their life or from their pain or symptoms.

These are obviously imaginary dialogues, and you won't know exactly what responses might occur in real life. Don't script these dialogues ahead of time, but rather allow them to unfold as they occur. A dialogue can uncover hidden truths about the source of MBS symptoms.

Most dialogues take about ten to fifteen minutes, but you can write as long as you need to. After each dialogue, write your affirmations in the space provided.

Letters to Yourself

After writing your dialogues this week, reflect on and write a description of what you have learned. This may include what you have learned from this person, event, or entity and in what ways you can see that you may have grown as a result of your relationship with him, her, or it. State how you've been able to deal with any issues related to the subject of your dialogue and how you plan on dealing in the future with any issues that have come to your attention or have been left behind from the past. See Progoff for more on dialogues (1975).

Week Three, Day One:

Identify who the speakers will be below and then write a dialogue chosen from the list. It is helpful to continue to write the name of each speaker preceding what he, she, or it says. Express your thoughts and feelings fully. Use as much paper as needed. Remember to allow the other person, event, or entity to respond to you fully as well.

Speaker 1 = _____

Speaker 2 = _____

The Dialogue

Complete this dialogue by writing the following affirmation—fill in the name of the person or entity with whom you conducted the dialogue—below three times:

I am grateful to explore and increase my understanding of my relationship with _____.

-

-

-

Reflect on the dialogue you wrote in a letter to yourself or to someone else.

What have you learned from this dialogue? In what ways have you gained from this interaction (even if there were very negative aspects of the relationship)? How have you been able to deal with any issues related to this relationship, and how do you plan on dealing with these issues in the future?

Dear _____,

Week Three, Day Two:

Create a dialogue in the space below.

Speaker 1 = _____

Speaker 2 = _____

The Dialogue

Complete this dialogue by writing the following affirmation—fill in the name of the person or entity with whom you conducted the dialogue—below three times:

I am grateful to explore and increase my understanding of my relationship with _____.

-

-

-

Reflect on the dialogue you wrote in a letter to yourself or to someone else. What have you learned from this dialogue? In what ways have you gained from this interaction (even if there were very negative aspects of the relationship)? How have you been able to deal with any issues related to this relationship, and how do you plan on dealing with these issues in the future?

Dear _____,

Week Three, Day Three:

Create a dialogue in the space below.

Speaker 1 = _____

Speaker 2 = _____

The Dialogue

Complete this dialogue by writing the following affirmation—fill in the name of the person or entity with whom you conducted the dialogue—below three times:

I am grateful to explore and increase my understanding of my relationship with _____.

-

-

-

Reflect on the dialogue you wrote in a letter to yourself or to someone else. What have you learned from this dialogue? In what ways have you gained from this interaction (even if there were very negative aspects of the relationship)? How have you been able to deal with any issues related to this relationship, and how do you plan on dealing with these issues in the future?

Dear _____,

Week Three, Day Four:

Create a dialogue in the space below.

Speaker 1 = _____

Speaker 2 = _____

The Dialogue

Complete this dialogue by writing the following affirmation—fill in the name of the person or entity with whom you conducted the dialogue—below three times:

I am grateful to explore and increase my understanding of my relationship with _____.

-

-

-

Reflect on the dialogue you wrote in a letter to yourself or to someone else.

Dear _____,

Week Three, Day Five:

Create a dialogue in the space below.

Speaker 1 = _____

Speaker 2 = _____

The Dialogue

Complete this dialogue by writing the following affirmation—fill in the name of the person or entity with whom you conducted the dialogue—below three times:

I am grateful to explore and increase my understanding of my relationship with _____.

-

-

-

Reflect on the dialogue you wrote in a letter to yourself or to someone else.

Dear _____,

Week Three, Day Six:

Create a dialogue in the space below.

Speaker 1 = _____

Speaker 2 = _____

The Dialogue

Complete this dialogue by writing the following affirmation—fill in the name of the person or entity with whom you conducted the dialogue—below three times:

I am grateful to explore and increase my understanding of my relationship

with _____.

-
-
-

Reflect on the dialogue you wrote in a letter to yourself or to someone else.

Dear _____,

Week Three, Day Seven:

Create a dialogue in the space below.

Speaker 1 = _____

Speaker 2 = _____

The Dialogue

Complete this dialogue by writing the following affirmation—fill in the name of the person or entity with whom you conducted the dialogue—below three times:

I am grateful to explore and increase my understanding of my relationship with _____.

-

-

-

Reflect on the dialogue you wrote in a letter to yourself or to someone else.

Dear _____,

Supplemental Writing Exercises for Week Three

In addition to the dialogues, the following exercises have been helpful in recovering from MBS. There are three lists to complete to prepare for writing.

Gratitude List

When you are in pain for any significant length of time, the pain and your problems often become all that you think about. Pain, thoughts about pain, and feelings about pain can easily take over your life to the point where there is nothing left. In order to rid yourself from pain, you need to be able to pay attention to the things in your life that are working and that are good. One step in this direction is to give thanks for the positives in your life.

Make a list of things for which you are grateful. Include anything you can think of—such as having a roof over your head, food to eat, the sun rising each day, a color, friends, family, etc. Consider including things for which you may be only partly grateful, for example, difficult people or things that may have taught you important lessons.

Gratitude List:

a. _____

b. _____

c. _____

d. _____

e. _____

f. _____

g. _____

h. _____

i. _____

j. _____

k. _____

l. _____

m. _____

n. _____

o. _____

p. _____

q. _____

r. _____

s. _____

t. _____

u. _____

v. _____

w. _____

x. _____

y. _____

z. _____

Forgiveness Lists

How many people do you know who hold grudges? Typically, a grudge is held as if it were a precious gem. We hang onto it tightly and guard it with ferocity. Holding onto strong feelings of anger and resentment towards others is harmful. It is like holding onto a poison which gradually saps us of health and power. Harboring resentment over long periods of time, especially if we don't acknowledge it, is often a major factor that perpetuates the vicious cycle of Mind Body Syndrome. Often there is nothing we can do about the situations that bother us. If there is no direct action we can take to resolve the situation, we are left with emotional pains that serve to exacerbate physical pain.

The only way out of this condition is forgiveness. Forgiveness is a gift that you give to yourself. It is an act which allows you to free yourself from the prison of toxic emotions. Learning to forgive means that you are letting go of the emotional pain you harbor and that you choose to stop allowing a situation from the past to harm you today. It doesn't mean that the other person was "right." It means you are taking steps to free yourself and prevent another person from controlling your reactions any longer.

When you decide to forgive someone or some entity, you are taking a powerful step towards your health and towards eliminating your pain. It is that simple and that important. I have seen many people who harbor anger towards someone who injured them, often in a car accident. Since the accident occurred many months or years ago, the body tissues have healed. What is causing their current pain is that the emotional wounds have not healed. And that is something they can control!

Forgiveness is often a necessary ingredient in cases where we harbor guilt over something we did or didn't do. As you now know, MBS frequently develops in those of us who are self-critical and who tend to feel guilty. I treated a woman who harbored deep guilt that stemmed from her daughter's violent death. She clung to the belief that she should have protected her daughter, despite the fact that this would have been impossible. Her pain was a way of punishing herself. Guilt is an extremely powerful emotion that is at the core of MBS in a large proportion of my patients. That is why forgiving yourself is a critical component of this program. You deserve forgiveness from yourself and from others. There are several scientific (McCullough, 2001) and lay books (Enright, 2001) that you can read for more information on forgiveness.

Make a list of the people that you would like to forgive for something they might have done. List people that you would like to ask for forgiveness for something you may have done. Finally, list those things for which you would like to forgive yourself.

Those you would like to forgive:

a. _____

b. _____

c. _____

d. _____

e. _____

f. _____

g. _____

h. _____

i. _____

j. _____

k. _____

l. _____

m. _____

Those you would like to ask for forgiveness:

a. _____

b. _____

c. _____

d. _____

e. _____

f. _____

g. _____

h. _____

i. _____

j. _____

k. _____

l. _____

m. _____

Things for which you would like to forgive yourself:

a. _____

b. _____

c. _____

d. _____

e. _____

f. _____

g. _____

h. _____

i _____

j. _____

k. _____

l. _____

m. _____

List of barriers to getting better

A common barrier to curing MBS is the way that the mind can adapt to being in pain for a long time. The pain can become part of our identity. And in a weird way, it becomes comfortable. The subconscious mind is so powerful that it can create a virtual prison for us. No one wants to be in pain. Yet there are often subconscious forces that create strong barriers to getting better.

I treated a woman who had severe pain for many years and when she started the course, her pain started to decrease. As soon as this happened, she began to feel anxious and had trouble sleeping. These are very common reactions that Freud termed symptom substitutions, situations where the mind will substitute new symptoms for old ones because it's not ready to give up having symptoms yet. It is also caused by the progress that one is making, because the mind is starting to give up the usual (old) symptoms. This woman came to the class in tears, crying these words: "I can't stand the anxiety and the sleeplessness. Give me my pain back! I'm at least used to my pain."

The subconscious mind can hang onto symptoms because these symptoms can help us avoid certain situations or get some things that we may need. If we maintain our symptoms, we may avoid having to work, to attend family functions, or fulfill certain social obligations. Some of these situations may cause us anger, fear, or anxiety. If we hang onto our symptoms, we may obtain sympathy or attention, or we may feel that we are very strong or a martyr. These are very common human reactions to life situations and to chronic symptoms. If we are brave enough and honest enough to look for these issues, we can begin to free ourselves of barriers that prevent us from getting better.

It takes a great deal of insight and courage to do this. I recall a woman who had the courage to state that she wasn't sure her husband would pay attention to her if she didn't have MBS symptoms. One man told me that a barrier for him was that if he did get better, it would mean that he actually could have gotten better several years earlier.

In the movie, *The Shawshank Redemption*, prisoners subjected to vicious and inhumane treatment when they enter prison learn to adapt to life inside the prison walls. Although consciously all of them proclaim their innocence and cannot wait to be set free, they are subconsciously affected by their physical prison and they gradually create a prison of their own within their minds. The film calls this "institutionalization," and the characters deal with this powerful force in different ways.

People in chronic pain are too often subjected to a process that can be termed "medicalization." Their experiences of chronic pain and many unsuccessful attempts to treat it can lead to a life where the only constant is pain.

Make a list of possible reasons why your mind might want to hang on to any MBS symptoms. Include things such as not having to work, not having to help with chores or family obligations, getting calls or sympathy from friends or family, etc. Do not be afraid that this list will harm you in any way. It is to uncover hidden reasons in the subconscious mind that might get in the way of ridding yourself of MBS symptoms. Everyone is likely to have some hidden barriers.

List of barriers:

a. _____

b. _____

c. _____

d. _____

e. _____

f. _____

g. _____

h. _____

i. _____

j. _____

k. _____

l. _____

m. _____

n. _____

o. _____

p. _____

q. _____

r. _____

s. _____

t. _____

u. _____

v. _____

w. _____

x. _____

Supplemental Writing Exercises: Gratitude, Forgiveness, Barriers

Choose topics that you think are important to you or that will help you get better from the gratitude, forgiveness, and barrier lists, and write them on the corresponding lines below.

Gratitude List Topics:

1. _____

2. _____

3. _____

Forgiveness List Topics:

1. _____

2. _____

3. _____

Barriers List Topics:

1. _____

2. _____

3. _____

Each day choose one of these topics and do a free-write exercise with the instructions on the following pages. There are pages for two fast writes for each category. Do as many as necessary from each of these categories on separate paper.

Gratefulness Free-Write No. 1

I am grateful for _____ and this is why:

Gratefulness Free-Write No. 2

I am grateful for _____ and this is why:

Forgiveness Free-Write No. 1

I forgive _____ for _____ and this is why:

    OR

I ask forgiveness from _____ for _____ and this is why:

    OR

I forgive myself for _____ and this is why:

Forgiveness Free-Write No. 2

I forgive _____ for _____ and this is why:

     OR

I ask forgiveness from _____ for _____ and this is why:

     OR

I forgive myself for _____ and this is why:

Barriers Free-Write No. 1

My mind may prefer to hang on to my symptoms because _____
_____

but this is why I choose to get better and this is how I'm going to overcome this barrier:

Barriers Free-Write No. 2

My mind may prefer to hang on to my symptoms because _____

_____

but this is why I choose to get better and this is how I'm going to overcome this barrier:

Meditation for Week Three: Dialogue with the Subconscious Mind

You will find the meditation for this week on the third track of the CD. The theme concerns a dialogue and fits in with the change in tone for this week's exercises. You will be moving towards an integration of your mind and body, having them work together for health and happiness. Begin this dialogue with your mind in the spirit of cooperation and harmony. Listen to the third track each day this week. You may also want to listen to either of the first two tracks as well, if you are able.

Meditation Synopsis

Find a spot where you will not be disturbed for several minutes. Start with the basic breathing techniques of noticing each breath, accepting it as it is, and letting each breath go. Notice that the subconscious mind is made up of everything that has occurred in the past, everything that is currently happening, and how it has reacted to these events. Recognize that the subconscious has a child-mind component and a parent-mind component. Recognize that the subconscious is not always rational, yet we are able to communicate with it. Gently ask the subconscious mind to stop causing the physical symptoms and emotional reactions that have occurred in the past. Tell the subconscious mind that you understand that it has been upset or hurt, but that you do not want to be in pain. Tell the subconscious child-mind that you will pay attention to it, but that you will not tolerate the development of any physical symptoms. Tell the subconscious parent-mind that you will pay attention to it, but that you will not tolerate the production of any physical symptoms. Picture the subconscious mind as a sea with rippling currents and small waves. When you instruct the subconscious to stop causing symptoms, picture the sea turning calm and quiet.

Picture your body as healthy. Picture every body part as functioning normally, able to participate in daily life without any significant pain or discomfort. Thank the subconscious mind for allowing the symptoms to diminish and disappear. Tell the subconscious that you will pay attention to it in the future so there is no real need for it to cause these symptoms to occur. Repeat to yourself three times, "I fully and completely accept myself. I let go of issues that have bothered me in the past. I choose to respond to my current stressors so they don't affect my health. I realize that I am not perfect, but I choose to accept my personality as it is, and I will not let any of these issues affect my health. I take

pride in doing this work, which helps me to be in control and to be more healthy in mind and body."

Reprogramming the Brain: Week Three Exercises

Review the week one and week two reprogramming exercises. Continue to use these exercises. However, for this third week, I suggest a slight change in how you do these. As you will notice, there is a progression in the design of the program. In the first week, you are asked to write freely about feelings and express them fully (before writing about how you understand them and where they come from) and you are asked to talk very forcefully (even yell) at the subconscious mind in order to take control of your symptoms. In the second week, you are asked to write unsent letters in which you can express anything that needs to be said, anything you need to get off your chest or tell someone (or yourself or a part of yourself). In the third week, you are asked to write dialogues. In these dialogues, you can express yourself, but you are also listening to what someone else or some part of you has to say. It is a two-way street, and you can learn to accept what others need to tell you or what you can see in yourself. This is an important step towards healing and growth.

Following this progression, reprogramming the brain exercises for the third week can change to become more accepting of yourself. Now, instead of yelling or screaming at the mind, you can gently ask your mind to stop doing what it has been doing in the past. You can gently laugh at yourself and at how the mind creates some of the symptoms. You can make friends with yourself and your subconscious mind, rather than be at war with it. The goal is to be whole and at peace with yourself. Work at being loving and accepting of yourself, and that includes accepting your internal child, your internal parent, your conscious mind, and your subconscious mind. Recognize that you're not perfect and that you may still continue to have MBS symptoms at times (I certainly do), but the more you can be kind to yourself and the more you can love and accept your whole self, the better you'll be able to fend off physical and psychological symptoms and become healthier and happier.

Another thing you can do is to reward your subconscious mind for "good" behavior. This, of course, is a classic way to retrain or reprogram. We started off the program with the "stick" of yelling at the subconscious and taking control away from it. You needed to establish that your conscious mind will be in charge and that you are going to change the patterns of pain and other symptoms that have been going on for so long. Often the subconscious mind will fight back because it is not ready to give up control just yet. That's why symptoms often worsen or move to other spots or morph into different symptoms. That's when you need to be very forceful to take control.

Now we are going to start using the "carrot" with the subconscious mind. Think of ways you can reward yourself and your subconscious mind. Make sure to thank the subconscious mind for getting better. Praise it, and tell it that it's doing a great job by letting go of old patterns and by learning new ones. Do more things that you enjoy. You will be rewarding yourself and your mind, and you will feel more whole as you make peace within yourself.

So, this week, work at being kind to yourself. When you talk to your mind and your body, speak more gently and laugh if you can at certain situations and triggers that produce symptoms. You may need to be forceful at times, of course. Feel free to do whatever is necessary to cause your symptoms to decrease. When you catch yourself having MBS symptoms, it can be similar to catching a beloved child with his hand in the cookie jar. You can chuckle at the child because he doesn't mean to be naughty; he was just trying to get away with something. Then tell the mind not to do that anymore, but you don't need to yell or punish it. You can correct it in a loving, positive way, as you would a child, knowing that you accept the subconscious as part of you and that it will learn.

Rebuilding Your Life: Make Commitments to Yourself

This week I invite you to engage in some specific activities that will help you in your recovery from MBS. You probably need to break some habits that have held you back. Many people are limited in what physical activities they do because of pain or fear of pain. In order to cure yourself, you will need to face these issues head-on and start to overcome them. Choose some activities to free yourself and move your recovery forward.

Choose to do some things that will make you happy. If you rarely do anything for yourself, it may be somewhat difficult to find things to do, but it is important that you act. Also, find some things to do for others, not out of obligation, but things that will also give you pleasure.

Finally, choose only those activities that you believe are most important to you and those that you believe you can actually carry out. Make a list of those activities below. List those things you are willing to make a commitment to doing.

Exercise: Things I Make a Commitment to Doing

Activities:

This week:

In the next month:

In the next six months to one year:

Things for myself:

This week:

In the next month:

In the next six months to one year:

Things for others:

This week:

In the next month:

In the next six months to one year:

Act on Your Commitments:

Now take the items in the above lists **that pertain to this week** and begin to plan for completing them. Take the ones that might be more difficult to accomplish, and use the following worksheets to help you figure out how to do them.

Worksheet for planning and carrying out commitments:

List the action _____

When do you plan on starting it? When do you plan on achieving it? _____
_____
_____

How will you accomplish it? What steps do you need to take? Which ones will you do first?
_____
_____
_____
_____
_____

What kind of help or aid will you need? Who can help you? What strategies will you need to use to achieve your goals? _____
_____
_____
_____
_____

What barriers might you encounter? How will you overcome them? _____
_____
_____
_____

I make a commitment to this activity by _____ (date).

Signed _____

Worksheet for planning and carrying out commitments:

List the action _____

When do you plan on starting it? When do you plan on achieving it? _____
_____
_____

How will you accomplish it? What steps do you need to take? Which ones will you do first?
_____
_____
_____
_____
_____

What kind of help or aid will you need? Who can help you? What strategies will you need to use to achieve your goals? _____
_____
_____
_____
_____

What barriers might you encounter? How will you overcome them? _____
_____
_____
_____

I make a commitment to this activity by _____ (date).

Signed _____

Worksheet for planning and carrying out commitments:

List the action _____

When do you plan on starting it? When do you plan on achieving it? _____
_____
_____

How will you accomplish it? What steps do you need to take? Which ones will you do first?
_____
_____
_____
_____
_____

What kind of help or aid will you need? Who can help you? What strategies will you need to use to achieve your goals? _____
_____
_____
_____
_____

What barriers might you encounter? How will you overcome them? _____
_____
_____
_____

I make a commitment to this activity by _____ (date).

Signed _____

If You Are Not Yet Improving

At this point in the program, some people begin to wonder if this approach will work for them, especially if they have not begun to see results. Although changes in pain often occur very quickly, there are also many people who don't experience these changes for a couple of weeks, or even a bit longer. If you have any concerns about the program at this point, please read the following.

1. Erase doubt.

Recognize that your true diagnosis is MBS and that the symptoms you are experiencing are completely due to the interaction between the mind and the body. If you begin to doubt if you truly have MBS or you begin to wonder if some other purely physical condition is present, you will be undermining your recovery by creating a subconscious barrier, as described in this chapter. Contact your doctor if you think some new physical condition has developed, but be aware that symptoms of MBS typically shift and move around when you start doing this work. If you are going to succeed in this program, it is essential to maintain an unwavering commitment to the understanding that your diagnosis is MBS and that by working in this way, you will succeed in getting rid of your symptoms.

2. Be patient.

Your symptoms have probably been present for a fairly long time. They may take some time to go away. Don't worry if you aren't seeing immediate results. If you keep working on the program, you will begin to see results. Don't try too hard, and don't get more stressed by worrying about doing the program perfectly. The program works very well, and you don't need to add more stress by worrying if you will get better. In fact, the more relaxed and confident you are, the quicker you will see results.

3. Keep working.

Continue to keep working on the program. Don't give up. Many people tend to avoid doing the homework, don't find the time, or procrastinate about it. This is another way that your mind can create barriers to recovery. Trust in this program, and trust in yourself. Choose the issues you think you need to work on, and use the writing and the meditations to deal with them. Make sure you do the reprogramming the brain exercises, and don't forget to take time for yourself.

4. Know thyself.

Be willing to look at your life and the things that have happened. Be willing to be honest with yourself. Everyone has done things they wish they hadn't or things they are ashamed of. Everyone has had things happen to them that they wish had never happened. It will help to recall these things and deal with them through the writing and meditating exercises. The more you are able to be honest with yourself and be kind to yourself, the more you will be able to accept yourself and let go of some of the stressful emotions that cause MBS symptoms. Practice being honest and kind with others as well.

5. Find contentment.

Find ways to be content or happy. Find things to be grateful for. Do things that you like and that give you pleasure. Find ways to relax. Do things for others that will give you happiness. Seek help from friends, family, co-workers, and counselors to gain support and understanding. Listen to others, and see if they will listen to you. Connecting to others in a deep way leads to an improved sense of self.

6. Do something.

Become more active. Challenge yourself physically by doing some things that you haven't done due to pain or fear. Complete your lists of activities you would like to do, and include some things that you can start doing immediately. The more active you are, the less time you will have to be in pain and the quicker you will get better.

chapter 10

Week Four: Creating the New You

Seize the very first possible opportunity to act on every resolution you make, and on every emotional prompting you may experience in the direction of habits you aspire to gain. — William James

Even though you may want to move forward in your life, you may have one foot on the brakes. In order to be free, we must learn how to let go. Release the hurt. Release the fear. Refuse to entertain your old pain. The energy it takes to hang onto the past is holding you back from a new life. What is it you would let go of today? — Mary Manin Morrissey

How do you feel about yourself? If you're like most people, you have a variety

of positive and negative thoughts about yourself, ranging from kind to disparaging. The way you talk to yourself can have great effects on how you are and what you do. You can choose how you see yourself and which aspects you emphasize in yourself. And once you begin to act in ways that emphasize the qualities you admire in yourself, those actions become habits that are easier to perform regularly. The more you act in ways that are consistent with how you'd like to be, your self image changes.

If you want to be kinder to yourself or to your family, you simply need to practice being kinder in small ways on a regular basis. If you want to be more assertive, practice saying "no" when asked to do something that you really don't want to do. If you want to be more generous or more outgoing, you can practice acting in those ways. If you want to be healthier, more active, or more fit, you can begin to do things that make you this way, and you will come to see yourself as a healthier, more active, and more fit person.

A good first step is to look inward to discover some positive qualities that you often ignore. There is an old story about a Native American elder who is telling his grandson about two creatures who are at war inside him: one a wild dog that is mean, vicious, and tells lies; the other an eagle that is kind, just, and honest. The small boy's eyes widen, and he asks his grandfather who will win this war. The elder statesman answers: "Whichever one I feed."

It is up to you to notice this "war" that occurs in you. You can choose to "feed"—to pay attention to and nourish—those qualities that move you in the direction you would like to travel. You can choose to live in anger, fear, guilt, and sadness, or you can live in love, hope, and joy. You make these choices daily. The more often you choose to live in love, hope, and joy, the more that will be who you are.

Exercise: Being Open to and Accepting of Yourself

Think for several moments about what you notice about yourself. Focus on the times when you are open, accepting, and kind to yourself—those times when the "eagle" is dominant. What do you notice when you are kind, open, and accepting of yourself? How do you feel at these times? How do you act towards yourself and others? On the lines below, write down anything that comes to mind in response to these questions. Examples might be "I feel happy" or "I notice calmness." Be patient, and see what thoughts arise. List as many items as you can.

_____

_____

_____

_____

_____

_____

_____

_____

_____

_____

_____

_____

_____

The way that you feel when you are open and accepting of yourself is entirely dependent on how you look at yourself. What would it be like to spend a day (or every day) filled with the feelings you listed above? Who controls if you feel open and accepting of yourself? You do. If you'd like to spend more time feeling like your list above, all you have to do is this: When you wake up each morning, make a decision to be open and accepting of yourself that day. Allow that concept to sink into your heart and mind every day. Feel some of the feelings that you listed above each morning and remind yourself of them throughout the day. Over time, it will tend to become the way you experience yourself and your life.

Now that you can see some of the positive characteristics that you already have within you, consider what other characteristics you would like to emphasize. You can also think about how you might be able to use some of these positive characteristics when you are faced with certain stressful situations. For example, how would you like to respond to a stressful conversation with a parent, child, sibling, friend, boss, or coworker? How would you like to respond to a frustration that arises? How would you like to respond to a flare-up of pain or other symptom?

List the characteristics that you would like to emphasize in your life:

(Examples might include being more kind to yourself, more outgoing, calmer, happier, more assertive, or worrying less)

_____

_____

_____

_____

_____

_____

_____

_____

_____

_____

_____

_____

_____

_____

_____

_____

Now make a list of stressful situations that you are probably going to encounter—including those you expect to occur in the next several weeks or months.

List of situations that are likely to be stressful: (Examples might include certain conversations, meetings, frustrations, symptoms)

_____

_____

_____

_____

_____

_____

_____

_____

_____

_____

_____

_____

_____

_____

_____

_____

_____

_____

_____

_____

Writing Exercise for Week Four: The New You Responds

From the lists you have just created, choose a characteristic or a situation that is important to you, and write about it. You can write from the point of view of the new you—how you will be, how you will act, how you will respond to certain situations in your life. Incorporate the characteristics you would like to emphasize in yourself, and write about how you will think and act to "feed" these characteristics. Do as many of these exercises as necessary to help you plan your responses. Then incorporate these responses into your life. Complete one of these exercises each day or every other day this week. Use extra paper if necessary.

The New You Responds No.1

_____ has just happened (or will happen soon). How will you respond? What characteristics will you bring to this situation? Write the story of this situation as you'd like it to play out with the new you as the prime actor.

The New You Responds No.2

_____ has just happened (or will happen soon). How will you respond? What characteristics will you bring to this situation? Write the story of this situation as you'd like it to play out with the new you as the prime actor.

The New You Responds No.3

_____ has just happened (or will happen soon). How will you respond? What characteristics will you bring to this situation? Write the story of this situation as you'd like it to play out with the new you as the prime actor.

The New You Responds No.4

_____ has just happened (or will happen soon). How will you respond? What characteristics will you bring to this situation? Write the story of this situation as you'd like it to play out with the new you as the prime actor.

The New You Responds No.5

_____ has just happened (or will happen soon).

How will you respond? What characteristics will you bring to this situation? Write the story of this

situation as you'd like it to play out with the new you as the prime actor.

Meditation for Week Four: Picturing the New You

Listen to this meditation, and take time to visualize each of the images. Several studies have demonstrated that visualization can have powerful effects on physical activities (Ross, et. al., 2003; Lacourse, et. al., 2005), overall health (Trakhtenberg, 2008), and pain (MacIver, et. al., 2008).

Meditation Synopsis

Take a few moments to place yourself in a comfortable situation where you won't be disturbed. Thank yourself for taking time for yourself and for doing this important work. Breathe deeply and allow yourself to relax. Observe your breath filling your lungs completely and watch as your lungs empty fully.

Picture the times when you are open and accepting of your self. Take a few moments and let these thoughts and feelings sink in. Ask yourself: "What do I notice when I am open and accepting of myself?" Pay close attention to these thoughts and these feelings as you answer this question.

Picture yourself going through a day being open and accepting of yourself. Picture how you would feel, how you would react to others, how you would react to events and situations.

Now take a few moments to consider some of the traits and characteristics that you would like to develop in yourself. Ask yourself these questions: "What characteristics would I like to have? What kind of person would I like to be?" Take some time to answer these questions, and let the answers sink into your mind.

Next, create an image of yourself doing something that you would like to do or that you have to do. Picture yourself as you make preparations for this and as you begin to do it. Make the images as vivid and real as you can.

Picture yourself doing this activity without any pain or dysfunction. Picture yourself completing this activity or task easily and effortlessly. See this clearly, and feel yourself as you would like to be.

Picture yourself as being the way you'd like to be throughout the day—how you feel, what you do, how you respond to people, situations, and events. What kinds of things would you do?

What kinds of things would you say? Create these actions and conversations in your mind.

Finally, take a few moments to think about things you would like to do in the future. Picture yourself overcoming any barriers to doing them. Picture yourself being healthier, stronger, and more able to do these things. Picture the new you as being happier, kinder, and more loving and forgiving to yourself and to others. Picture yourself being grateful for the things you have in your life.

End this session with these wishes for yourself:

"May I be peaceful and contented,

May I be free from harm and illness,

May I be loving and loved,

May I be forgiving and forgiven."

Repeat these wishes three times.

Think of others in your life who might benefit from these wishes or others to whom you would like to send these wishes. Repeat these wishes for these people three times.

"May they be peaceful and contented,

May they be free from harm and illness,

May they be loving and loved,

May they be forgiving and forgiven."

Dealing with Difficult Situations

You are probably aware of some issues or situations that are unfinished and still bother you. These may involve business situations where money is owed or relationships where feelings were hurt. Conflicts often occur between people which are left unresolved for many years.

Make a list of things that you need to do, finish, resolve, or take care of. On this list, place anything that still weighs on your mind, even if you're not sure you can do anything to resolve it, and even if doing something about it would be very difficult or even impossible.

In one of my classes, there was a married woman who was diagnosed with fibromyalgia and had a tremendous amount of physical pain. A major stressor was that her sister-in-law was spreading false rumors that she was having an affair. When she came to this point in the program, she decided to confront her sister-in-law. They met, and she explained that she was not having an affair and told her to stop spreading the rumors. Within days, her pain melted away.

Sometimes we just need to act—by doing certain exercises or work, by pushing our bodies to do things we have been avoiding, by expressing ourselves to others, or by changing our work or a relationship situation in some way.

Make a list of:

Things that you need to do,

Things that you should take care of,

Things that are important for you to resolve (even if they may be difficult)

_____

_____

_____

_____

_____

_____

_____

_____

_____

_____

_____

_____

_____

_____

_____

_____

_____

_____

_____

_____

_____

_____

Choose two or three items from this list and decide what you might be able to do about them. At this time, you might only be able to do a free-write on the subject to begin to recognize your feelings. Or you just may be able to write an unsent letter. You might be able to write a letter and send it or call the person involved and discuss the issue. You might be able to meet with the person and apologize or ask for forgiveness. You might need to ask someone to do something that needs to be done. You may need to make up your mind and take action.

Write one item from your list on this line _____

Consider what you could do about this in the next week or two. Write those options on the following lines.

_____

_____

_____

_____

_____

_____

_____

_____

_____

_____

_____

_____

_____

Choose an initial plan of action. Write it here.

_____

_____

_____

_____

_____

_____

Set a deadline for accomplishing this task in the next week or two.

_____

Figure out how you're going to accomplish this task. Who can help you? Who can you ask for advice? Can someone go with you? How are you going to accomplish the task? What barriers might occur, and how will you overcome them?

Write a paragraph answering these questions.

Make a commitment to this task. Even though these tasks may be very difficult, most people feel much better after they accomplish them. Even if your first step is a small one, it will often give you the courage and confidence to take a slightly larger step if the issue is still unresolved.

After you have accomplished your task, write a brief paragraph describing what happened, how you felt, and what this accomplished.

Now that you've accomplished one small task on this issue, was this enough to help you resolve or finish this issue? Do you need to take a further step? Or can you move on to another issue that needs to be resolved?

Consider what this next step might be and go through the same process as you did before. Remember that while taking these steps can be difficult, the results are almost always positive and you will feel better both emotionally and physically when you have been able to complete these tasks.

Choose another issue that needs resolving, and write that item from your list on this line.

_____

Consider what you could do about this in the next week or two. Write those options on the following lines.

_____

_____

_____

_____

_____

_____

_____

_____

_____

Choose an initial plan of action. Write it here.

_____

_____

_____

_____

_____

_____

Set a deadline for accomplishing this task in the next week or two.

_____

Figure out how you're going to accomplish this task. Who can help you? Who can you ask for advice? Can someone go with you? How are you going to accomplish the task? What barriers might occur, and how will you overcome them?

Write a paragraph answering these questions.

Make a commitment to this task. Even though these tasks may be difficult, most people feel much better after they accomplish them. Even if your first step is a small one, it will often give you the courage and confidence to take a slightly larger step if the issue is still unresolved.

After you have accomplished your task, write a brief paragraph describing what happened, how you felt, and what this accomplished.

Now that you've accomplished one small task on this issue, was this enough to help you resolve or finish this issue? Do you need to take a further step? Or can you move on to another issue that needs to be resolved?

Consider what this next step might be, and go through the same process as you did before. Remember that while taking these steps can be very difficult, the results are almost always positive and you will feel better both emotionally and physically when you have been able to complete these tasks.

Choose another issue that needs resolving, and write that item from your list on this line.

_____

Consider what you could do about this in the next week or two. Write those options on the following lines.

_____

_____

_____

_____

_____

_____

_____

_____

_____

_____

_____

Choose an initial plan of action. Write it here.

_____

_____

_____

_____

_____

_____

Set a deadline for accomplishing this task in the next week or two.

Figure out how you're going to accomplish this task. Who can help you? Who can you ask for advice? Can someone go with you? How are you going to accomplish the task? What barriers might occur, and how will you overcome them?

Write a paragraph answering these questions.

Make a commitment to this task. Even though these tasks may be very difficult, most people feel much better after they accomplish them. Even if your first step is a small one, it will often give you the courage and confidence to take a slightly larger step if the issue is still unresolved.

After you have accomplished your task, write a brief paragraph describing what happened, how you felt, and what this accomplished.

Writing Exercise: Write Your Life Story in a New Way

Everyone has a narrative or a story they tell themselves about their lives. These stories are very powerful, not only because they remind us of our past but because they also affect our future, since to a large degree we tend to think what we can accomplish is controlled by what happened in our past. However, there are many ways to view the past and many opportunities to alter our futures. This exercise gives you the opportunity to create a new life story.

Your Old Story:

First, write a synopsis or short version of your old story: the one where you emphasize the negative things that have happened in your life and how you tend to be limited by this view of yourself. In this version, we frequently see ourselves as a victim of sorts—bad things happen to us, and we are unable to change them or rise above them. Keep this relatively short because you don't want to dwell on it.

Your New Story:

Now, write a new story for yourself. You can take the facts about things that have occurred, but try to put a new twist on them. Write about what you have learned from them and how you have (or will) overcome significant stressors or barriers. Emphasize the positive things that have happened to you and your positive reactions to life events. Emphasize your successes and things you have accomplished. This is an opportunity to view yourself as a hero—someone who has faced great odds yet finds a way to overcome them and triumph. If you can look at your life as a "hero's journey," you will be better equipped to deal with adversity and to change your life in important ways.

As you do this exercise, you will be creating the person you would like to be. Create the person who you really are: able to make new choices, able to overcome past problems, able to accomplish the things that you would like to accomplish.

chapter 11

Next Steps: Charting Your Future

Now I become myself. It's taken
Time, many years and places;
I have been dissolved and shaken,
Worn other people's faces… — May Sarton

When you get into a tight place and everything
goes against you until it seems that you cannot hold on
for a minute longer, never give up then, for that is
just the place and time when the tide will turn. — Harriet Beecher Stowe

You are now finishing the four-week program, and you can be proud of all the hard work you've done. Hopefully, you've learned a great deal about Mind Body Syndrome and how it has impacted your life. You have probably discovered many things about yourself along the way. This program is designed not only to help you understand MBS and conquer it, but to take more control of your life and take steps toward a better future. What steps will help you improve further? Some of you have already seen great progress in reducing or eliminating your MBS symptoms. For others, you may have found only limited improvement to date. This chapter gives guidance on how to proceed in either of these situations.

For Those Yet to Complete Their Recovery

Not everyone who does this program will find relief quickly. MBS can be tricky sometimes. Our minds can find ways to thwart our progress and cling to MBS symptoms.

Do not despair or give up. If you dwell in negativity, you activate the anterior cingulate cortex, the part of the brain that perpetuates pain. Stay as positive as you can. Remember that the pain pathways probably developed a long time ago, and it may take a while to overcome them. It's worth another few weeks or months to get better if you know you are on the right path. For some people, it takes up to a year for their brains to be rewired and their pain to resolve.

One of the most important and common barriers to getting better is the persistent belief that there is something physically wrong with your body. You might think, "Maybe I really have a problem with my back from that injury," or "Maybe the doctors missed something on their exam or their testing," or "I wonder if I should get another medical opinion." If you have thoughts such as these, it is critical to deal with them quickly. To get better, you must be completely certain that your symptoms are caused by MBS—doubt can lead to fear and/or despair. If you are not sure that you have MBS, seek out doctors who can carefully review your situation, your exam, and your testing. See the Appendix for a doctor who has experience in MBS, or you can see a doctor in your area that you trust. (You might want to have your doctor read the first few chapters of this book.)

If you are confident that you do have MBS, you have several options. One is to start the program over. This is a good option for people who have many psychological issues in their lives and need more time to address them and for those who haven't had time to complete the exercises. Restarting also provides clear guidance and structure. It may take a few more weeks of working on the psychological issues and on talking to your mind and your body for the message of MBS to really become integrated and accepted.

If you are a perfectionist, however, it may not be a good idea to restart the program from the beginning. Overly conscientious people with high expectations of themselves may work so hard on the program that it puts added pressure on them, preventing them from getting better. Other people find they are writing about the same psychological issues over and over and feel stuck in a rut. For such people, it is best to take a break from the structured program for a while and follow the rest of the advice in this section.

Another approach is to pick and choose the exercises that you'd like to complete over the next few weeks—those that give you the best opportunity to work on particular issues in ways you find helpful. Feel free to do so, especially if you feel you have made some progress.

What barriers might be preventing you from getting better? Maybe you haven't yet identified some important psychological issues that are causing your mind to continue to produce pain signals.

To determine if there are specific barriers you may have missed, review chapter 9. It's very common for some hidden parts of you to prefer NOT to get better. Identify those potential barriers and complete the writing exercises to address them. You may also need to work on them with the reprogramming the brain affirmations and the meditations.

It's very common for people to have issues in their lives they've avoided addressing, especially ones that make them uncomfortable. Who would want to confront an angry neighbor or boss? Why rehash issues from many years ago with a sister or brother? Wouldn't it be better to forget an issue with a parent or religious leader that goes back all the way to your childhood? What is the benefit of returning to a place where trauma began? And why uncover feelings that are emotionally difficult to deal with?

MBS is often caused by deep, suppressed emotions that need to be resolved in order to undo the pain. It's not always enough to write about or meditate on some of these issues. It is frequently necessary to do something actively to resolve them. If this might be the case for you, review chapter 10 and consider beginning this sometimes difficult work. One man had to speak with his father about some issues that had caused tremendous strife many years earlier. A woman found that she had to make a very difficult decision about her son. He had been taking advantage of her for several years, lying and stealing money from her to pay for his drug addiction. She couldn't bring herself to separate from him. But when she did, this is what she wrote:

> In order to heal yourself from fibromyalgia and other MBS symptoms, you have to look at the truth in your life, no matter what it is. If you live an illusion, you will never reach the end you seek. In this program, I have learned the truth about my life and myself. I have learned things that I needed to learn and have made difficult, yet important, decisions about my life and my relationships. To have health in our bodies, our minds need to be at peace. As I have found peace, I find I like myself more and I find that my body is healthy again. Thanks to this program, my bodily pain, my headaches, and my fatigue are so much better.

One of the biggest barriers to getting better is anxiety and fear. You may fear that your symptoms will never get better or that new ones may develop. But if you live in fear, you are more likely to stay in pain and develop new MBS symptoms. Many people have been told by doctors or physical therapists that there is something wrong with their back or neck or joints. They have been warned to be extremely careful in lifting, bending, or running. They live in fear. It is critical to realize that your pain cannot harm you. If you live in fear of pain, you will not get better. You must be able to accept that pain occurs and not panic when it does. You must learn to relax and have confidence that your pain will go away. Know that you are healthy and on the right path. Work to banish worry, fear, and anxiety by using the same techniques that you applied to your pain. Write to the worry, talk to the fear, and meditate on the anxiety.

One woman who had severe pain found that this was a key to getting better. She wrote:

Something pretty profound happened this last week. The pain nearly went away. I was able to create some wiggle room in my mind to stop thinking about the pain and actually BELIEVE myself capable of being pain-free and VISUALIZE myself engaged in my activity with ease. I did some pretty intense physical exercise with very little symptoms. Some "soreness" was still there the next day, but I nonetheless repeated what I did with courage, not fear, and again, I moved through pretty intense activity with very little discomfort. Why? Trust. All of a sudden, I actually let go. I said to myself, pain or no pain, I am trusting life. If it gives pain, there are still lessons to learn; when I am without pain, it is time to celebrate and be present—not fear what is not there. I also tell myself throughout the day that I am strong, healthy, and at ease in my body—and then visualize my body full of light, moving with grace, confidence and ease. If I shift my attention to my heart and go through my day from a place of trust, no matter how I feel, it is OK. I feel that I can reconnect with trusting life and surrendering. I am practicing those skills (patience, relaxation, gratitude, health) that are the opposite of the traits (worry, fear, distrust) that produce MBS pain.

These are key words to live by: trust, courage, confidence, relaxation, belief, and being comfortable in your own body and in your own life every moment. If you meet fear and anxiety with calmness and ease, and if you know deep down that you are healthy and strong, you will be fine. It takes repetition for the brain to develop new pathways, so you need to keep repeating to yourself: "I am strong and healthy. I can do whatever I choose. I am not afraid. I am confident and calm."

Do as many activities as you can do, and expand them so that you are proving to yourself that you are healthy and strong. One man who had severe pain in both thighs for over twenty years couldn't walk more than ten feet before he had to stop due to excruciating pain. However, he was determined to conquer his pain, and he was absolutely sure that he had MBS and nothing more. He started by walking ten feet and resting—and walking ten more feet. Over the course of a couple of weeks, he could walk fifteen feet, then twenty. As he increased his exercise, his pain became a bit more tolerable, and he realized he was on the right track. He is now pain free and able to walk as much as he likes. Each person needs to figure out how much activity is best and how quickly to increase it. You may want to work with a trainer or take a physical activity class in order to have someone guide you. The more active you are, the quicker you will retrain your brain and develop new non-pain pathways.

For some people, the best thing to do after finishing this program is to take a break from it. The emotional work is significant and can be stressful. Make sure to be kind to yourself and to take time for yourself. It's a critical element in your healing process. If you have not been able to do so, try again to find time for activities for yourself—a minimum of four to five hours per week on fun and pleasurable activities. Keep experimenting until you find something that delights you. It can be walking, riding a bike, knitting, bowling, golf, collecting, shopping, meeting friends for lunch, planning a trip, or anything that gives you joy. If you have to force yourself to do this, it's probably all the more important that you do so.

Another powerful option is to stop focusing on the inward journey and begin to focus more on the external. At some point, it is necessary to balance the hard and long work you've done on your MBS with work for others, for family and community. At times, we can get so wrapped up in our own issues that we neglect to move forward with our lives. So many people have had to put their lives on hold due to chronic pain that a critical element in healing is getting back to living your life. You may decide that you really need to get back to work or exercise or volunteering or connecting to others. These positive, life-affirming activities will help you experience happiness and make contributions to others, as well as yourself. An older woman was living alone and suffering greatly with chronic back pain. After finishing the program, she moved to an assisted living residence and began to engage in new friendships and activities. As she became less isolated and happier, her pain vanished.

This program places a great deal of emphasis on reflection and meditation as components of healing. I've been a teacher of mindfulness meditation for more than fifteen years. For people attracted to meditation, I strongly recommend it as a way to continue to investigate and resolve life issues and improve health. Mindfulness meditation can be used throughout the day and is very helpful in dealing with chronic pain (Gardner-Nix, 2009). There are mindfulness meditation teachers all over the world who offer courses and retreats. See www.umassmed.edu/cfm/mbsr to find a program in your area. Ronald Siegel, Psy.D., has an excellent book (*The Mindfulness Solution*, 2010) and a website with several free meditations on it (www.mindfulness-solutions.com).

Another resource I recommend is the work of Byron Katie. She has several books, including

Loving What Is (2002), and a great website, www.thework.org. Those materials have been invaluable for many of my patients. Several have found relief from their MBS symptoms after viewing her online videos, reading her books, and taking her common-sense advice to heart. Key elements to this work are compassion and forgiveness for oneself and others. Those who have experienced difficult childhoods often feel undeserving of love. They may even blame themselves for being a victim of traumatic events. For people in this situation, recovery from MBS is often dependent on learning love and forgiveness for self. Two excellent resources in this regard are *The Mindful Path to Self Compassion* (Germer, 2009) and *The Love Response* (Selhub, 2009).

There are also hypnosis and imagery tools that can be extremely helpful. For example, Belleruth Naparstek, Emmett Miller, MD, and several other leaders in the field of mind body medicine have produced CDs that contain visual imagery, relaxation, and hypnotic suggestions designed to calm the mind and allow the body to heal. See www.healthjourneys.com for information on specific CDs that are available for help with healing back pain, headaches, and other forms of Mind Body Syndrome.

As you now understand, at the core of Mind Body Syndrome are emotions that have been held onto and haven't been adequately expressed or released. Many of the exercises in this book are geared towards accessing these emotions. However, it may be difficult to identify them or pay enough attention to them in order to heal. It is a natural reflex for most people to suppress or ignore strong emotions. I have developed another meditation for the purpose of helping people directly experience deep emotions in a way that helps to allow expression and release. You can find this meditation at www.unlearnyourpain.com/mbs-book. Click on Embracing Emotions meditation as an aid to directly experience fear, anxiety, sadness, anger, or gulit with less resistance, in order to deactivate and release these powerful emotions.

Finally, many people with persistent MBS symptoms enter into a relationship with a psychologist or counselor that they trust. Individuals with MBS who have depression, anxiety, post-traumatic stress disorder, obsessive-compulsive disorder, eating disorders, and other psychological issues can benefit from counseling and/or medication.

Because the underlying cause of MBS is usually rooted in early childhood emotions, it is very helpful to find a psychologist or therapist who is familiar with these types of problems. A list of therapists with expertise and interest in MBS is in the Appendix. Some conduct therapy over the phone. Choosing a therapist is an important decision; interview them about their knowledge of MBS prior to engaging in a long-term relationship. Ask if they will read this book or review web sites (see the Appendix) so they know how you'd like to approach your problems.

Life coaching is another way that some people learn to resolve their symptoms. There are some coaches who work over the phone or online who are skilled and knowledgeable regarding MBS (also listed in the Appendix).

In working with a therapist or coach, continue to explore the relationships between psychological issues and physical events. Our bodies are very sensitive to changes in our minds and reflect those changes on a day-to-day (and even minute-to-minute) basis. When you develop an increase in an MBS symptom or a new MBS symptom, there is a reason for it. Your body speaks to you, but it doesn't have verbal language for communication. It will alert you that something is bothering you by creating a physical (or a psychological) symptom. Listen to it, and discover why it is creating these symptoms whenever they occur. MBS can be viewed as a guide to help you heal your life.

A young woman wrote the following:

Strange as it may sound, I am thankful for my experience with Mind Body Syndrome. Without the incentive from that wretched pain, I never would have looked inside myself for the answers. In doing so, I was forced to confront old demons and begin the path towards healing, both inside and out.

MBS is treatable and curable. For some, it takes quite awhile and a lot of work. But it is well worth it, so do not give up! The work you do will help you understand yourself and free you from being tied to reactions to emotions. It will help you live the life that you choose to live.

Once You Have Recovered

Those people who have had dramatic improvements in their MBS symptoms are usually extremely relieved that finally something has worked. They are typically amazed that a relatively simple program could actually take away their pain, and that reactions within the mind could cause their symptoms.

Even if your symptoms are now mild or nonexistent, there are several things you still may want to accomplish. You may want to keep working and learning about yourself. The exercises in this program have proven to be very helpful in dealing with stressful events and emotional reactions.

Consider continuing to do them in some way, whether keeping a diary, writing unsent letters or dialogues, or meditating regularly. Use the affirmations and continue to remind yourself that you're healthy, strong, and able to withstand stressful events. Keep this book handy and visible, so that you remember to use these exercises when you need them.

At times, you may develop some amount of recurrent pain or some new MBS symptom. The reason is simple: you are still human. All of our minds and bodies are intimately connected. Since your body serves as a built-in alarm system, it will alert you when things that are occurring in your life are troubling, even if you are not aware that you are upset. Of course, if you get new symptoms, you want to make sure there is nothing physically wrong. You may need to see your doctor to be sure. However, since you understand MBS, you will want to look for issues in your life as a cause for new symptoms. Often it is easy to identify them when you take a few minutes to think. The earlier you identify new symptoms as being due to MBS, the quicker you can stop them from taking hold. Often times, an unsent letter, a meditation, some affirmations, or some exercise can stop new MBS symptoms in their tracks! It is important to remain confident that you are, in fact, healthy and strong and able to conquer any new MBS symptoms. With that attitude, you will be able to maintain freedom from MBS over the long haul.

Finally, you may want to help others. Once you learn about MBS, you will realize that some of your friends and relatives suffer from it. Naturally, you'd like to help them and you'll want to tell them about how their symptoms can be cured if properly understood. However, be forewarned: Most people you tell about this will not be interested, or they will refuse to think that their condition could be MBS. This is a natural consequence of the way that modern medicine approaches physical symptoms. Few doctors are aware of MBS and even fewer patients. Many people's initial reaction to hearing about MBS is that they are being accused of being weak, or crazy, or faking their pain, or that their symptoms are all in their head. They may not understand that people with MBS are just normal people who have emotional reactions to stress.

More doctors and patients need to understand MBS. If they did, many people could be saved from years of suffering, and we would be a healthier society. If there were fewer stigmas attached to the idea that the mind can cause real pain and other symptoms, more people would get the kind of help they really need, rather than receiving medical testing and treatment that is ineffective or even harmful. In addition, health care costs would decline by eliminating unnecessary testing and treatments. You can help by educating your doctor and your friends and family about MBS. In the future,

I hope that we will more frequently see this kind of interaction in a doctor's office: "So, I see you've started having back pain (or headaches or stomach pain). I'm going to examine you to make sure there is no sign of a serious medical condition. Then I'd like to ask you a bit about what's been going on in your life."

chapter 12

Frequently Asked Questions

What if pain, the kind that opens a fist, is really the tap of an angel saving us from ourselves? —Mark Nepo

What about asthma, ulcerative colitis, or rheumatoid arthritis? Can these be forms of Mind Body Syndrome?

I generally divide disorders into three categories. Disorders that occur more frequently as people age are primarily degenerative physical conditions, such as cancer, strokes, and heart attacks. These are not caused by thoughts or emotions, nor can they reliably be cured by changing our thoughts and emotions. A second category of illnesses are those which occur in younger people, have clear evidence of tissue destruction, yet also seem to be significantly influenced by the mind. These disorders include asthma, ulcerative colitis, Crohn's disease, multiple sclerosis, rheumatoid arthritis, and other immune-related disorders. There is no evidence that changing the mind can reliably cure these disorders, and I would not expect that any tissue destruction that has already occurred will be reversed. However, it is possible that this program can help to reduce or eliminate exacerbations of these disorders. The third category of disorder is Mind Body Syndrome in all of its varied manifestations.

I have read that migraine headaches and fibromyalgia are genetic diseases. If that is true, how can they be caused by Mind Body Syndrome?

It is clear that we are not born with a "clean slate." Everyone is born with certain genes for hair, skin, eye color, ability in music and athletics, and general temperament. It has been shown that some people are born with a higher likelihood of being fearful and introverted, while others are more extroverted and risk-taking. Some people have the misfortune to be born with genes that cause them to have specific diseases, such as cystic fibrosis, sickle-cell anemia, or Tay-Sachs disease. Some genes will cause specific disorders, while others simply lead to a higher likelihood of a certain condition. Those genes in the latter group can be "turned on" or "turned off" during our lifetime.

In migraine headaches, fibromyalgia, anxiety, and other disorders that I include under Mind Body Syndrome, genetic factors account for only 15 to 40 percent of the likelihood of developing these disorders. In other words, those genes do not "cause" those disorders, but they can make a person more likely to develop them if they are put in the situation in their life that triggers MBS. The genes associated with MBS will not cause the disorder to occur unless they are turned on by stressful events in childhood and by the occurrence of emotional stressors later in life. The term used for this phenomenon is epigenetics, and a good lay explanation of this can be found in *The Biology of Belief* (Lipton, 2008). When you educate yourself about MBS and take the steps in your life to unlearn your pain, those genes will be turned off.

I get the impression from what I have read that understanding MBS processes is all that is necessary for healing MBS. For me, this does not seem to be enough. Undertanding the process and uncovering the unconscious traumas or stressors seems to be only part of the puzzle, because this has not led to improvement in my symptoms.

In my experience, knowledge about MBS is enough to eliminate pain in approximately 10 to 15 percent of patients. Everyone else needs to figure out how to identify and deal with the psychological issues causing pain. MBS is caused by unresolved emotions, and it is usually necessary to resolve them to get better.

Many people need to make changes in their lives. It often takes a great deal of courage to face the situations that hold us hostage. But we must face those situations and deal with them directly and honestly. While it is true that many situations are unchangeable, we can still cope with them better, understand them better, learn to live with them or accept them, and learn to find the grace and lessons that they teach us. Many situations can be changed, however, and we can make the decisions needed to change them.

Everyone gets pain from time to time. How will I know if a pain is really MBS or something that requires medical attention? Do I need to be concerned that I'll hurt myself if I exercise again?

There is no way to be 100 percent sure if an acute pain is really MBS or an injury. Here are some clues that an acute pain is actually caused by MBS: it occurs without an injury, it occurs when another MBS pain gets better, and/or it occurs after some stress or emotion. For a pain that occurs while running or exercising, it is often hard to know for sure. If it heals within a few days or so, it was probably a mild injury that just needed time to heal. If it persists for a longer time than expected for a mild injury, then it is probably MBS. If you build up the amount of exercise you do gradually, you should have no problem, as long as you keep reminding your body that it is strong and healthy and that it can tolerate exercise without any problems.

Why is it so important to believe that the program will work? What if I'm skeptical? Will that undermine my likelihood of success?

I'm often a skeptic myself, particularly about expensive medical treatments that don't make biological sense and that make the patient dependent on the doctor. This program is different because it's based on solid scientific research about how pain develops and persists.

All treatment regimens—including exercise, medications, and surgery—work better if the patient believes in them. That's the well-known placebo effect. But this program is more than a placebo. This program works because it addresses the actual underlying reason for the pain. This is just good medicine: finding the source of the problem and dealing with it in a straightforward and powerful manner.

It's fine to have a healthy amount of skepticism. Many people have gotten better despite being skeptical that this program would work for them. But it will be difficult to be cured if you don't believe that MBS explains why you have your pain. Chronic pain and other MBS symptoms are caused by nerve pathways which have been learned in response to significant emotional issues and have been reinforced over a significant amount of time. These nerve pathways are primarily contained in the subconscious mind and are reinforced by worry, fear, and uncertainty. If you believe a physical problem is causing your pain, this gives the subconscious mind an "out," a way to continue producing pain.

In order to unlearn your pain, you must clearly understand that the source of the pain is due to MBS, that negative normal emotional reactions to stress have caused the pain, and that mental processes can reverse the pain.

Should I stop taking my pain medications for this program to work? What about my medication for depression or anxiety?

It is fine to take medication for pain, anxiety, or depression while you are working on the MBS program. If you are in severe pain, it can be very difficult to participate in this program, so pain medications are often necessary. Do not stop any medications without first speaking to your physician. After your pain or anxiety or depression gets better, you can taper off your medication, in consultation with your physician. If you stop your medication too early, your mind can use that as an excuse to cause your MBS symptoms to recur.

I have been told I need physical therapy in order to stretch and strengthen my body. Should I continue it, or will that deflect attention from the MBS to something "physical?" What about exercise? How much should I do?

I encourage all my patients to exercise, get stronger, and learn to trust their bodies. It would be wrong to run on a fractured ankle. But with MBS, there is no fracture and no physical damage, and therefore there should be no fear of injury. What holds people back is pain and fear of pain. So, work through the fear and pain by gradually increasing the amount of exercise that you do.

Physical therapy is a form of exercise, so I have no problem with that. While you are exercising, make sure to tell yourself frequently that your body is strong, you are healthy, there is nothing wrong with your body, and that you are doing this to get stronger. If your physical therapist reinforces the idea that there is something wrong with your muscles or joints, this can delay your recovery from MBS. If you can't find a physical therapist who understands MBS, consider a personal trainer to help you get stronger and more flexible.

Some days I have a couple of hours a day to spend on the program, but some days I don't have any time. Is it OK to work on one week's material for two weeks rather than one?

You can go at your own pace. If you can complete the program in two months rather than one, that's perfectly fine. I don't want people who are very busy to overwork themselves and put extra stress into their lives. So, find a good balance. But be sure to make time to work on the program so that you get its benefit. You deserve to get better, and you need to take time in order to do the work that's required.

How do I deal with people who doubt the MBS concept? They are always telling me to go to the doctor again to see if there is a physical problem. This makes me doubt myself, and then I find that my pain is worse.

People always do better in the MBS program when they are convinced that their physical and psychological problems are due to stress and reactions to stress. But we will sometimes wonder if we're on the right track. A woman recently told me that she must have something physically wrong because her pain was so severe, even though her pain had lessened after one week of this program. These kinds of doubts are common and will arise in most people.

It is critical to realize that thoughts are uncontrollable. We don't choose what thoughts come into our heads. The mind will continually come up with a wide variety of thoughts, many of which are unproductive, weird, or even inane. If we can't control our own thoughts, we certainly cannot control other people's thoughts, and therefore we must learn ways of reacting to thoughts or else we will be at the mercy of every stray thought that we (or someone else) comes up with. Of course, we also need to deal with emotions, which are often connected to important material from our past.

An excellent way to deal with thoughts and emotions is by practicing mindfulness. The first meditation in chapter 7 provides the basics of mindfulness. This practice teaches us to be aware of thoughts and emotions without having to react to them, without having our bodies react to them, and without allowing the mind to cause pain or other physical symptoms as it has done in the past. See chapter 11 for other helpful resources.

If thoughts (such as doubts) can cause you to have increased pain or other physical symptoms, that confirms that those symptoms are due to MBS. With regard to doubt about having a physical condition, if you have had a good medical evaluation and there are no significant findings on your physical and neurological examination, you most likely have MBS. Your mind is an incredible trickster and will keep you in pain as long as you let it. The solution is to be convinced that you have MBS and to be powerful in fighting it. Be persistent and believe in yourself, and you'll be fine.

I'm just starting my first week of this course and have a question about reprogramming the mind. I think this is a key to my recovery as I've identified some strong triggers that I have not been able to keep from causing my symptoms in the past. Most of the triggers are involved with work, and they make doing my job difficult while also causing me fear. How can I deal with these triggers?

First, it is important to realize that triggers are things that can initiate symptoms, but they are not directly causing them. When Pavlov's dogs salivated at the sound of the buzzer, it triggered the symptoms only because that nerve pathway was learned by their brain. The trigger can be extinguished over time by disconnecting the buzzer from the food. In your case, it would be helpful to figure out why work is a trigger for you. Is it because your symptoms started at work, because you are in, or have been in, difficult situations there, because you do certain activities at work that may seem to cause pain, or all of the above?

Second, you need to look at any issues that are occurring at work and figure out if you can continue to work there and what you can do to change things. If you decide to continue working at this job, you will need to find ways of stopping your pain at work. Persistently talk to yourself prior to going to work, while entering work, and at work. Tell your mind that your body doesn't need to have these symptoms anymore. Tell it, forcefully and clearly, to stop producing them. Get immersed in your job, stay focused on doing the very best you can. Focus on enjoying any aspects of the job that you can, and being grateful for having a job. The more content you are in your situation, the better able you will be to stop the vicious cycle of nerve connections that have formed.

Finally, you need to learn to relax and not worry if symptoms develop. The more you worry, the more you will trigger the symptoms, because the symptoms feed on your emotions. You've had symptoms before, and they may be uncomfortable—but they won't harm you, because there is no physical disease. You will survive, and you will get better. Be confident that you are on the mend and getting better. Listen to the first week's meditation and train yourself to accept what is happening now, and learn to let thoughts, emotions, and body sensations go. Then focus on something else, anything else, such as your breath, your elbow, your surroundings, some music, or your work. In this way, you are reprogramming your brain away from the nerve connections that cause symptoms.

After starting the program, I am finding that my symptoms are getting worse. Am I doing something wrong? This has made be anxious, and that seems to make my pain worse. I'm also feeling depressed and tired. Should I stop the program or go slower with it?

It is common for symptoms to become worse or for new symptoms to emerge when starting the program, especially with the writing exercises. There are several reasons for this. First, you are uncovering emotions that have been buried. This is a healthy process, but also one that often leads in the short run to strong feelings, such as worry, fear, sadness, or guilt. Second, your mind is going to realize that you are finally catching onto the fact that the physical symptoms are due to unresolved emotions. Therefore, it will tend to create other symptoms to keep you off track or scare you into stopping this work. The new symptoms can be physical or psychological ones, such as anxiety, fatigue, or depression. You have done nothing wrong; in fact, when this work causes your symptoms to change you are clearly on the right track. Don't give up because this is actually a sign that you are making progress. If you need pain or anxiety medication for the short term, that's fine; don't worry about taking it. You can always stop when you don't need it anymore.

You may also want to consider seeing a counselor. You are absolutely correct that anxiety can cause and exacerbate pain. So, keep writing, meditating, and doing the affirmations. Tell your pain to leave and begin to talk to the anxiety with the same message. They are both manifestations of MBS, so treat them the same way. As for depression and fatigue, your mind is trying to give you the message that this work is too hard or too scary. Don't allow your mind to get away with that. Stopping would be giving in to your subconscious mind, which wants to stay in control and avoid change. Write to the negativity and depression; talk to it. Tell it that you know what it's trying to do. As the course progresses, you will begin to overcome those issues, to see them in a new light, to learn from them, and learn to let them go.

I'm either waking up in the middle of the night or I wake up with pain. How can I deal with those things which are occurring while I sleep?

When you sleep, your conscious brain is sleeping, while your subconscious mind is not only awake, but fully in charge. It is necessary to deal with your subconscious in order to stop sleep from being a trigger for your symptoms. Before you go to bed each night, write out a list of the things on your mind and leave it next to the bed (or somewhere else if you prefer). Write at the bottom of the list, "I'll deal with these tomorrow. I will not worry about them at all tonight while I sleep." Then do one of the meditations in this program, a visualization (see chapter 11 for these resources), or listen to some soft music. Finally, before you fall asleep, firmly instruct your mind that you're going to sleep fully and completely all night; that you will not worry about any of your problems tonight; and most importantly, that you are going to wake up with no pain. Do this each night for two weeks, and you will sleep better and your morning pain will lessen or go away.

I was doing really well when I started the program. My pain was going down, and I was beginning to feel good for the first time in several years. Then my pain returned, and now it seems worse than ever. What did I do wrong? I'm worried that it won't go away again and that I'll be stuck back where I was. What should I do?

First, you should realize that you have been successful with this program. You saw a decrease in your pain simply by thinking about it differently and beginning to do the psychological exercises. That should reassure you that you can get better.

You should also understand that setbacks do occur in most people. They happen because the brain and the body are deeply interconnected. Subconscious emotions and thoughts can easily trigger pain or other MBS symptoms. You may not even be able to figure out what thoughts or emotions caused the reactivation of pain. You may have started to be more active and then your body said, "Hold on, there; not so fast." The mind and body are used to having pain, and it often takes some time to unlearn the nerve pathways that have developed. I still get MBS symptoms at times, and sometimes it is not clear what stress or thoughts bring it on. Here's how to turn it around.

First, be kind to yourself. Don't beat yourself up or blame yourself for this setback. And even though you are in pain, it is critical that you remain certain that MBS is the cause and that you can overcome it. Relax and take some deep breaths; collect yourself; do not let fear overtake you, because that can lead to more pain. Then take some time to try to figure out what triggered the pain. If you can't, don't worry, just go back to doing the things that led to your initial success. Keep reminding yourself that you are healthy and strong and that this is a temporary setback. Tell yourself that you will be fine soon. Be assertive, and continue to do more physical activities. Do the writing and the meditations. Don't fall into seeing yourself as a victim. Develop confidence in yourself and in your ability to heal yourself. This shall pass, and you will be fine.

One aspect of your program advises people to talk to their pain and to assertively tell it to go away. However, you also teach mindfulness meditation techniques, which suggest that one accepts the pain. Aren't these contradictory messages?

This is often seen as a conflict. It is important to challenge the pain and to work at reducing it by taking control. However, you can't go around yelling at yourself all the time. In addition, you don't want to be reacting to the pain all of the time. It's important to learn to relax and accept the moment as it is. If you're in pain, you're in pain right now. Mindfulness teaches you to react less strongly to pain. The typical reaction to pain is fear and worry, which causes pain to be worse. So, it's a balancing act. Learn to take control and get rid of the pain, but also accept that it's here now and that it can't harm you. Relax and have confidence that you'll beat it soon.

Why does my mind come up with new symptoms when I get rid of one of the old ones? When will it give up?

Once you recognize that the mind often creates substitute symptoms, you will be amazed at the variety of symptoms that may occur. This is a fascinating process to observe. it is very common to see pain move from one area to another or morph into fatigue or OCD symptoms. Most physicians don't understand this process, because it doesn't fit into their purely biomedical view of the body. One woman reported that her physician became angry with her when she reported that her pain kept shifting from one shoulder to the other.

When this process occurs, you can be sure of three things. The diagnosis of MBS is confirmed, because a structural problem in one area would not move around like that. If a particular symptom can disappear for a while that tells you that this symptom can definitely get better. Symptom substitution is a positive sign, as I frequently say: "You've got it on the run!"

The mind will continue to produce new symptoms or substitute symptoms for a variety of reasons. One, it's not quite ready to give up yet. If your symptoms have been there for a long time, it may take a bit longer for the brain to "get the message." Two, you haven't yet integrated the changes that you need to make in your life or in your psyche. Three, you haven't yet accepted yourself fully and completely—you are still fighting yourself, doubting yourself, being afraid of symptoms or of certain issues or events in your life. Four, you haven't yet learned what you need to learn from your symptoms. This may sound odd, but several people in the program have directly asked their symptoms (in meditation or in writing) this question, "What do I need to learn from you?"

Continue to be firm with your mind. Don't let if off the hook by worrying if a new symptom is really MBS or not. Don't doubt yourself. You are on the right track. Continue the process of writing, meditating, talking to your brain, and making changes in your life. Almost everyone gets symptom substitution, and if you're able to recognize it quickly and even laugh at the new symptom ("Isn't that funny that my body thinks it can get away with trying that one?"), then you're more likely to rid yourself of MBS symptoms soon.

How do I deal with anxiety? I worry if I'm going to get better and if this pain will come back.

The longer I am involved in this work, the more I see the key relationship between fear, worry, and anxiety and pain. What often happens is that the mind uses anxiety as a symptom substitution—it creates worry and fear when we catch on to the fact that the pain is caused by MBS. This is actually progress, because when anxiety occurs, it means that emotions are less suppressed. Now you can focus on dealing with the fear, worry, and anxiety. Accept that you have these feelings at times; and recognize that there are reasons for them and that they are normal. Then treat the anxiety just as you have learned to treat the pain. Notice it without getting upset, tell it that you know what is causing it, and tell it to go away.

In time, you'll see that the anxiety will begin to lose its power over you; you won't have to fight it or worry that it will cause terrible problems. Listen to the meditation for week one where I talk about noticing thoughts, accepting them as "just thoughts," and letting them go. You can treat fear and anxiety the same way: notice without judging, understand, accept, and let go. The more you feel these feelings without judging them, without fighting them, without worrying that they are a threat, the more you will be able to accept them and let them go. There is also an excellent meditation entitled Stepping into Fear, on Ronald Siegel's website: www.mindfulness-solution.com. Finally, listen to the Embracing Emotions meditation at www.unlearnyourpain.com/mbs-book.

You talk about forgiveness, but isn't that condoning what someone else did?

Forgiveness has little to do with other people. Whether they deserve to be forgiven is irrelevant. If you felt they deserved to be forgiven, you probably would have forgiven them a long time ago. But if you are not able to either forget or forgive, you are allowing the other person to control you and continue to hurt you. So, you are basically deciding to hurt yourself. Is this what you want? Is your anger so important that you will allow it to consume you and continue to cause pain?

Forgiveness doesn't mean that you like what happened, or that you think that was the right thing for someone to do. It means that you accept that it happened. It means that you realize that other people do things for their own reasons and that you have to take care of yourself. It means that you refuse to be controlled or defined by someone else's actions. It means that you are ready to move on and not wallow in anger or defeat. It also means that you realize that the other person was doing the best they could or the only thing they could do at the time.

When you forgive someone, it asserts your power to choose how you think and how you act. It means letting go of the past and learning that you are in control of your thoughts and your life. It is not an act of weakness, but one of strength.

appendix: additional resources

Books for Understanding and Healing MBS

MEDICAL BOOKS:

The Adaptive Unconscious – Timothy Wilson, PhD

Back Sense – Ronald Siegel, PsyD, Michael Urdang, Douglas Johnson, MD

The Biology of Belief – Bruce Lipton, PhD

Brain Lock – Jeffrey Schwartz, MD

The Brain that Changes Itself – Norman Doidge, MD

The Divided Mind – John Sarno, MD

The Emotional Brain – Joseph LeDoux, PhD

Emotions Revealed – Paul Ekman, PhD

Freedom From Fibromyalgia – Nancy Selfridge, MD

From Paralysis to Fatigue: A History of Psychosomatic Medicine – Edward Shorter, PhD

The Illusion of Conscious Will – Daniel Wegner, PhD

The Mindbody Prescription – John Sarno, MD

The Mindful Brain – Daniel Siegel, MD

Overtreated – Shannon Brownlee

Snake Oil Science – R. Barker Bausell, PhD

Stabbed in the Back – Nortin Hadler, MD

Stumbling onto Happiness – Daniel Gilbert, PhD

They Can't Find Anything Wrong – David Clarke, MD

Train Your Mind, Change Your Brain – Sharon Begley

SELF HELP BOOKS:

The Beggar King and the Secret of Happiness – Joel ben Izzy

Facing the Fire – John Lee

Full Catastrophe Living – Jon Kabat-Zinn, PhD

The Journey: A Practical Guide to Healing Your Life and Setting Yourself Free – Brandon Bays

The Love Response – Eva Selhub, MD

Loving What Is – Byron Katie

The Mindfulness Path to Self-Compassion – Christopher Germer, PhD

The Mindfulness Solution – Ronald Siegel, PsyD

The Places that Scare You – Pema Chodron

The Power of Now – Eckhart Tolle

The Presence Process – Michael Brown

Sanity, Insanity, and Common Sense – Enrique Suarez

The Secret Code of Success – Noah St. John

Slowing Down to the Speed of Life – Joe Bailey

The Spirituality of Imperfection: Storytelling and the Search for Meaning – Ernest Kurtz and Katherine Ketcham

Waking the Tiger: Healing Trauma – Peter Levine

What to Say When You Talk to Yourself – Shad Helmstetter

You Can Be Happy No Matter What – Richard Carlson

Health Professionals

USA, BY STATE:

CALIFORNIA

Arnold Bloch, LCSW
5655 N. Lindero Canyon Rd., Suite 704
West Lake Village, CA 91362
    and
10516 Santa Monica Blvd., Suite 2
Los Angeles, CA 90025
(805) 796-9540

Bruce Eisendorf, MD
2025 Soquel Avenue
Santa Cruz, CA 95062
www.scruzmedical.com
(831) 458-5524

Alan Gordon, LCSW
1247 7th St., Suite 300
Santa Monica, CA 90401
(310) 945-6811
    and
8500 Wilshire Blvd., Suite 705
Beverly Hills, CA 90211
(310) 945-6811

Helene G. Green, LCSW
19710 Ventura Blvd., Suite 203
Woodland Hills, CA 91364
(818) 999-9664

Philip S. Green, PhD
19710 Ventura Blvd., Suite 203
Woodland Hills, CA 91364
(818) 999-9663

Susan Mendenhall, MSW, PsyD
10111 McConnell Place
Los Angeles, CA 90064
(310) 558-8091

Colleen Perry, MFT
1247 7th Street #300
Santa Monica, CA 90401
(310) 259-8970
www.colleenperry.com

David Schechter, MD
8530 Wilshire Boulevard, Suite 250
Beverly Hills, CA 90211
(310) 657-0366
    and
3855 Hughes Avenue, Suite 200
Culver City, CA 90232
(310) 838-2225
www.mindbodymedicine.com

Clive M Segil, MD
2080 Century Park East, Suite 500
Los Angeles, CA 90067
(310) 203-5490

Nancy Sokolow, LCSW
530 Wilshire Blvd., Suite 310
Santa Monica, CA 90401
(310) 393-2020

Jill Solomon, MFT
8240 Beverly Blvd., Suite 8
Los Angeles, CA 90048
(323) 692-3759

Patti D. Thomas, LCSW
Peaceful Sea Counseling
920 Samoa Blvd., Suite 209
Arcata, CA 95521
(707) 822-0370
pdthomas@reninet.com

CONNECTICUT

Leslie Reis, LCSW
75 Kings Highway Cutoff
Fairfield, CT 06824
(203) 333-1133

Dario M. Zagar, MD
Associated Neurologists of
Southern Connecticut
75 Kings Highway Cutoff
Fairfield, CT 06824
(203) 333-1133
www.anscneuro.com

DISTRICT OF COLUMBIA

Andrea Leonard-Segal, MD
George Washington University Center
for Integrative Medicine, Suite 200
908 New Hampshire Avenue, N.W.
Washington, D.C. 20037
(202) 833-5055

GEORGIA

David Lipsig, MD
12 Piedmont Center, Suite 410
Atlanta, GA 30305
(404) 495-5900
Fax (404) 495-5901
www.atlantapsychiatry.com

Leonard J. Weiss, MD
3188 Atlanta Road
Smyrna, GA 30080
(770) 319-6000

ILLINOIS

John Stracks, MD
Northwestern Memorial Physicians
Group Center for Integrative Medicine
and Wellness
1100 E. Huron Street, Suite 1100
Chicago, IL 60611
(312) 926-DOCS (3627)

MARYLAND

Harold Goodman, DO
8609 Second Avenue, Suite 405-B
Silver Spring, Maryland 20910
(301) 565-2494
hrpharold@gmail.com

MASSACHUSETTS

Eugenio Martinez, MD
Greater Boston Orthopedic Center
200 Providence Highway
Dedham, MA 02026
(781) 461-4543
Fax (781) 326-2030.

Jay E. Rosenfeld, MD
311 Service Road
East Sandwich, MA 02537
(508) 833-4000
jrosenfeld@adelphia.net

Ronald D. Siegel, PsyD
20 Long Meadow Road
Lincoln, MA 01773
(781) 259-3434
www.backsense.org

MICHIGAN
Roger Gietzen, MD
1460 Walton Boulevard, Suite 200
Rochester Hills, MI 48309
(248) 650-1800
Fax (248) 650-1856

Howard Schubiner, MD
Providence Hospital
Department of Internal Medicine
16001 W. Nine Mile Road
Southfield, MI 48075
(248) 849-4728
hschubiner@gmail.com
www.unlearnyourpain.com

MINNESOTA
Douglas Hoffman, MD
St. Mary's / Duluth Clinic Health System
400 E. Third St.
Duluth, MN 55805
(218) 786-3520

NEW HAMPSHIRE
Marc Sopher, MD.
27 Hampton Road
Exeter, NH 03833
(603) 772-5684
Fax (603) 772-5256
mdsophermd@comcast.net
www.themindbodysyndrome.com

NEW JERSEY
Robert Paul Evans, PhD
163 Engle Street
Englewood, N. J. 07631
(201) 569-3328

Paul Gwozdz, MD
710 Easton Avenue, Suite 1A
Somerset, NJ 08873
(732) 545-4100
www.GwozdzMD.com

Thomas Nordstrom, M.D.
The Center for Orthopedic Care
215 Union Avenue
Bridgewater, New Jersey 08807
(908) 685-8500
Fax (908) 685-8009
www.tcfoc.com

NEW YORK
Frances Sommer Anderson, PhD
140 East 40th Street #12A
New York, New York 10016
(212) 661-7588

Ira Rashbaum, MD
Rusk Institute of Rehabilitation
Medicine
400 East 34th Street
New York, NY 10016
(212) 263-6328

John Sarno, MD
Rusk Institute of Rehabilitation
Medicine
400 East 34th Street
New York, NY 10016
www.healingbackpain.com
(212) 263-6035

Eric Sherman, PsyD
19 West 34th Street, Suite PH-13
New York, New York 10001
(212) 947-7111 x227

Roy Stern, MD
Dermatologist
800A Fifth Avenue, Suite 403
New York, NY 10021
(212) 421-SKIN (7546)

NORTH CAROLINA
Bruce Hill, MD
Crossroads Arthritis Center
300 Billingsley Road
Charlotte, NC 28211-1075
(704) 333-1400

OHIO
John Nadas, MD
1330 Mercy Dr NW, Suite 320
Canton, OH 44708
(330) 489-1495

Peter Zafirides, M.D. Psychiatry
5151 Reed Rd., Suite 128C
Columbus, OH 43220
(614) 538-8300
  and
Southeast Mental Health
16 W. Long Street
Columbus, OH 43215
(614) 225-0985

PENNSYLVANIA
Randy A. Cohen, DO
Pain Medicine and Rehabilitation
Specialists
160 North Pointe Boulevard, Suite 115
Lancaster, PA 17601
(717) 560-4480
Fax (717) 560-4485
rcohen@painstoppers.org

TENNESSEE
Christopher Vinsant, MD
501 16th Street, Suite 606
Knoxville, TN 37916

TEXAS
Jonna Lee Barta, PhD
101 W. McDermott Street, Suite 109
Allen, Texas 75013
jonna.barta@sbcglobal.net

John Sklar, MD
2500 West Freeway, Suite 400
Fort Worth, TX 76102
(817) 870-1868

WASHINGTON
Gail DiBernardo, MSW
22613 23rd Place West
Brier, Washington 98036
(425) 775-8820

Mark G Strom, MD
1370 Stewart Street, Suite 202
Seattle, WA 98109
(425) 922-7576
Fax (425) 669-7500
www.integrativehealthmd.com
mark@integrativehealthmd.com

WISCONSIN
Luke Fortney, M.D.
UW Integrative Medicine Program
621 Science Drive
Madison, WI 53711
(608) 262-9355
(800) 323-8942
luke.fortney@fammed.wisc.edu

UNITED KINGDOM:
Georgina Oldfield, MCSP
Chartered Physiotherapist
Pain Relief Centre, West Yorkshire, UK
00(44)1484 452500
info@tmsrecovery.com
www.tmsrecovery.com

Dr Nicholas Straiton FRCS, DM-S
Med, MLCOM
1 Glovers Yard, 121 Havelock Road
Brighton, BN1 6GN, UK
01273 540303
Fax 01273 540092
nicstraiton@btinternet.com

Life Coaches

Mona Grayson:
www.questionthemind.com

Monte Hueftle:
www.runningpain.com

Art Smith, PhD:
drsmith@noetichealth.com

Abigail Steidley:
www.thehealthylifecoach.com

Websites and Blogs:

Dave Clarke, MD
www.stressillness.com

Kim Ruby
www.tarpityoga.com/tms.html

Howard Schubiner, MD
www.unlearnyourpain.com

Marc Sopher, MD
www.tms-mindbodymedicine.com

David Schechter, MD
www.mindbodymedicine.com

TMS Help Forum
http://www.tmshelp.com/

TMS Wiki
www.tmswiki.org

references

Alesci S, Martinez PE, Kelkar S, Ilias I, Ronsaville DS, Listwak SJ, Ayala AR, Licinio J, Gold HK, Kling MA, Chrousos GP, Gold PW. Major depression is associated with significant diurnal elevations in plasma interleukin-6 levels, a shift of its circadian rhythm, and loss of physiological complexity in its secretion: clinical implications. *Journal of Clinical Endocrinology and Metabolism*. 2005, 90: 2522-30.

Amir M, Kaplan Z, Neumann L, Sharabani R, Shani N, Buskila D. Post-traumatic stress disorder, tenderness and fibromyalgia. *Journal of Psychosomatic Research*. 1997, 42: 607-613.

Anda RF, Felitti VJ, Bremner JD, Walker JD, Whitfield C, Perry BD, Dube SR, Giles WH. The enduring effects of abuse and related adverse experiences in childhood: A convergence of evidence from neurobiology and epidemiology. *European Archives of Psychiatry and Clinical Neuroscience*. 2006, 256: 174-86.

Arborelius L, Eklund MB. Both long and brief maternal separation produces persistent changes in tissue levels of brain monoamines in middle-aged female rats. *Neuroscience*. 2007, 145: 738-750.

Asmundson GJG, Katz J. Understanding the co-occurrence of anxiety disorders and chronic pain. State of the art. *Depression and Anxiety*. 2009, 26: 888-901.

Assor A, Roth G, Deci EL. The emotional costs of parents' conditional regard: A self-determination theory analysis. *Journal of Personality*. 2004, 72. 47-88.

Aubert A. Psychosocial stress, emotions and cytokine-related disorders. *Recent Patterns on Inflammation and Allergy Drug Discovery*. 2008, 2: 139-148.

Bailey KM, Carleton RN, Ylaeyen JWS, Asmundson GJG. Treatments addressing pain-related fear and anxiety in patients with chronic musculoskeletal pain: A preliminary review. *Cognitive Behaviour Therapy*. 2009, epub. August 20, 2009.

Bandura A. *Self-efficacy: The Exercise of Control*. W. H. Freeman, New York, NY. 1997.

Baranauskas G. Pain-induced plasticity in the spinal cord. In *Toward a Theory of Neuroplasticity*. Shaw CA and McEachern JC (eds.). Psychology Press, Philadelphia, PA. 2001.

Bargh JA, Pietromonaco P. Automatic information processing and social perception: The influence of trait information presented outside of conscious awareness on impression formation. *Journal of Personality and Social Psychology*. 1982, 43: 437-449.

Bargh JA. Auto-motives: Preconscious determinants of social interaction. In *Handbook of Motivation and Cognition*, T. Higgins and R. M. Sorrentino (eds.). Guilford Press. New York, NY. 1990.

Bargh JA, Chen M, Burrows L. Automaticity of social behavior: Direct effects of trait construct and stereotype activation on action. *Journal of Personality and Social Psychology*. 1996, 71: 230-244.

Baumgartner E, Finckh A, Cedraschi C, Vischer T. A six year prospective study of a cohort of patients with fibromyalgia. *Annals of Rheumatologic Diseases*. 2002, 61: 644-5.

Bausell, RB. *Snake Oil Science: The truth about complementary and alternative medicine*. Oxford University Press, New York, NY. 2007.

Beckham JC, Crawford AL, Feldman ME, Kirby AC, Hertzberg MA, Davidson JR, Moore SD. Chronic posttraumatic stress disorder and chronic pain in Vietnam combat veterans. *Journal of Psychosomatic Research*. 1997, 43: 379-389.

Begley S. *Train Your Mind, Change Your Brain*. Random House, New York, NY. 2008.

Boos N, Semmer N, Elfering A, Schade V, Gal I, Zanetti M, Kissling R, Buchegger N, Hodler J, Main CJ. Natural history of individuals with asymptomatic disc abnormalities in magnetic resonance imaging: predictors of low back pain-related medical consultation and work incapacity. *Spine*. 2000, 25: 1484-92.

Borenstein DG, O'Mara JW Jr, Boden SD, Lauerman WC, Jacobson A, Platenberg C, Schellinger D, Wiesel SW. The value of magnetic resonance imaging of the lumbar spine to predict low-back pain in asymptomatic subjects: a seven-year follow-up study. *Journal of Bone and Joint Surgery (American)* 2001, 83-A: 1306-11.

Brody H and Brody D. *The Placebo Response: How you can release the body's inner pharmacy*. HarperCollins Publishers, New York, NY. 2001.

Brownlee S. *Overtreated: Why too much medicine is making us sicker and poorer*. Bloomsbury USA, New York, NY. 2007.

Burns JW. Arousal of negative emotions and symptom-specific reactivity in chronic low back pain patients. *Emotion*. 2006, 6: 309-19.

Burns JW, Quartana P, Gilliam W, Gray E, Matsuura J, Nappi C, Wolfe B, Lofland K. Effects of anger suppression on pain severity and pain behaviors among chronic pain patients: evaluation of an ironic process model. *Health Psychology*. 2008, 27: 645-652.

Carragee EJ. Clinical practice. Persistent low back pain. *New England Journal of Medicine*. 2005, 352: 1891-8.

Castro WH, Meyer SJ, Becke ME, Nentwig CG, Hein MF, Ercan BI, Thomann S, Wessels U, Du Chesne AE. No stress—no whiplash? Prevalence of "whiplash" symptoms following exposure to a placebo rear-end collision. *International Journal of Legal Medicine*. 2001, 114: 316-22.

Celiker R, Borman P, Oktem F, Gokce-Kutsal Y, Basgoze O. Psychological disturbance in fibromyalgia: relation to pain severity. *Clinical Rheumatology*. 1997, 16: 179-184.

Christakis NA and Fowler JH. The spread of obesity in a large social network over 32 years. *New England Journal of Medicine*. 2007, 357: 370-379.

Christakis NA and Fowler JH. The collective dynamics of smoking in a large social network. *New England Journal of Medicine*. 2008, 358: 2249-2258.

Clarke DD. *They can't find anything wrong: 7 keys to understanding, treating, and healing stress*. First Sentient Publications, Boulder, CO. 2007.

Cohen N, Ader R, Green N, Bovbjerg D. Conditioned suppression of a thymus-independent antibody response. *Psychosomatic Medicine*. 1979, 41: 487-91.

Cohen H, Neumann L, Haiman Y, Matar MA, Buskila D. Prevalence of post-traumatic stress disorder in fibromyalgia patients: overlapping syndrome or post-traumatic fibromyalgia syndrome? *Seminars in Arthritis and Rheumatism*. 2002, 32: 38-50.

Costa PT Jr, Terracciano A, McCrae RR. Gender differences in personality traits across cultures: robust and surprising findings. *Journal of Personality and Social Psychology*. 2001, 81: 322-31.

Crombag HFM, Wagenaar WA, van Koppen PJ. Crashing memories and the problem of 'source monitoring.' *Applied Cognitive Psychology*. 1996,10: 95–104.

Cunningham A. Ivan Pavlov and the conditioning of physiological responses. *Advances in Mind Body Medicine*. 2001,17: 7-8.

Das P, Kemp AH, Liddell BJ, Brown KJ, Olivier G, Peduto A, Gordon E, Williams LM. Pathways for fear perception: modulation of amygdala activity by thalamo-cortical systems. *Neuroimage*. 2005, 26: 141-148.

Derbyshire SWG, Whalley MG, Stenger VA, Oakley DA. Cerebral activation during hypnotically induced and imagined pain. *Neuroimage*. 2004, 23: 392– 401.

Deyo RA, Rainville J, Kent DL. What can the history and physical examination tell us about low back pain? *Journal of the American Medical Association*. 1992, 268: 760-5.

Deyo RA, Mirza SK, Turner JA, Martin BI. Overtreating chronic back pain: time to back off? *Journal of the American Board of Family Medicine*. 2009, 22: 62-8.

Doidge N. *The Brain that Changes Itself*. Penguin Books, New York, NY. 2007.

Eisenberger NI, Jarcho JM, Lieberman MD, Naliboff BD. An experimental study of shared sensitivity to physical pain and social rejection. *Pain*. 2006, 126: 132-138.

Eisenberger NI, Lieberman MD, Williams KD. Does rejection hurt? An fMRI study of social exclusion. *Science*. 2003, 302: 290-292.

Enright RD. *Forgiveness is a choice*. American Psychological Association, Washington, DC. 2001.

Fitzgerald KD, Welsh RC, Gehring WJ, Abelson JL, Himle JA, Liberzon I, Taylor SF. Error-related hyperactivity of the anterior cingulate cortex in obsessive-compulsive disorder. *Biological Psychiatry*. 2005, 57: 287-94.

Flor H, Elbert T, Knecht S, Wienbruch C, Pantev C, Birbaumer N, Larbig W, Taub E. Phantom-limb pain as a perceptual correlate of cortical reorganization following arm amputation. *Nature*. 1995, 375: 482-4.

Fowler JH and Christakis NA. The dynamic spread of happiness in a large social network: longitudinal analysis over 20 years in the Framingham heart study. *British Medical Journal*. 2008, 337: a2338 (doi: 10.1136/bmj.a2338).

Freud S, Strachey J. *Sigmund Freud: The ego and the id*. W. W. Norton and Co., New York, NY. 1960.

Gardner-Nix J. *The Mindfulness Solution to Pain: Step-by-step techniques for chronic pain management*. New Harbinger Publications, Oakland, CA. 2009.

Gatchel RJ, Polatin PB, Mayer TG. The dominant role of psychosocial risk factors in the development of chronic low back pain disability. *Spine*. 1995, 20: 2702-9.

Geisser ME, Strader Donnell C, Petzke F, Gracely RH, Clauw DJ, Williams DA. Comorbid somatic symptoms and functional status in patients with fibromyalgia and chronic fatigue syndrome: sensory amplification as a common mechanism. *Psychosomatics*. 2008, 49: 235-42.

Germer C. *The Mindful Path to Self-Compassion: Freeing yourself from destructive thoughts and emotions*. The Guilford Press, New York, NY. 2009.

Giesecke T, Gracely RH, Grant MA, Nachemson A, Petzke F, Williams DA, Clauw DJ. Evidence of augmented central pain processing in idiopathic chronic low back pain. *Arthritis and Rheumatism*. 2004; 50: 613-623.

Goebel MU, Trebst AE, Steiner J, Xie YF, Exton MS, Frede S, Canbay AE, Michel MC, Heemann U, Schedlowski M. Behavioral conditioning of immunosuppression is possible in humans. *Federation of American Societies for Experimental Biology Journal*. 2002, 16: 1869-73.

Goldberg N. *Writing Down the Bones: Freeing the writer within*. Shambala Press, Boston, MA. 1986.

Goldberg RT, Pachas WN, Keith D. Relationship between traumatic events in childhood and chronic pain. *Disability and Rehabilitation*. 1999, 21: 23-30.

Goldenberg DL, Burckhardt C, Crofford L. Management of fibromyalgia syndrome. *Journal of the American Medical Association*. 2004, 292: 2388-95.

Gracely RH, Petzke F, Wolf JM, Clauw DJ. Functional magnetic resonance imaging evidence of augmented pain processing in fibromyalgia. *Arthritis and Rheumatism*. 2002, 46: 1333-43.

Grossman P, Tiefenthaler-Gilmer U, Raysz A, Kesper U. Mindfulness training as an intervention for fibromyalgia: evidence of postintervention and 3-year follow-up benefits in well-being. *Psychotherapy and Psychosomatics*. 2007, 76: 226-233.

Harriman PL. A case of hysterical paralysis. *Journal of Abnormal Psychology*. 1935, 29: 455-456.

Hooley JM, Gruber SA, Scott LA, Hiller JB, Yurgelun-Todd DA. Activation in dorsolateral prefrontal cortex in response to maternal criticism and praise in recovered depressed and healthy control participants. *Biological Psychiatry*. 2005, 57: 809-12.

Hsu MC, Schubiner H, Lumley MA, Stracks JS, Clauw DJ, Williams DA. Sustained pain reduction through affective self-awareness in fibromyalgia: a randomized controlled trial. (manuscript submitted)

Illich I. *Medical nemesis: the expropriation of health*. Pantheon Press, New York, NY. 1976.

James, W. What is an emotion? *Mind*, 1884, 9: 188-205.

Jensen MC, Brant-Zawadzki MN, Obuchowski N, Modic MT, Malkasian D, Ross JS. Magnetic resonance imaging of the lumbar spine in people without back pain. *New England Journal of Medicine*. 1994, 331: 69-73.

Kabat-Zinn J. An outpatient program in behavioral medicine for chronic pain patients based on the practice of mindfulness meditation: Theoretical considerations and preliminary results. *General Hospital Psychiatry.* 1982, 4: 33-47.

Katie B. *Loving What Is.* Three Rivers Press, New York, NY. 2002.

Keller RB, Atlas SJ, Soule DN, Singer DE, Deyo RA. Relationship between rates and outcomes of operative treatment for lumbar disc herniation and spinal stenosis. *Journal of Bone and Joint Surgery.* 1999, 81: 752-762.

Kirsch, I. Response expectancy as a determinant of experience and behavior. *American Psychologist.* 1985, 11: 1189-1202.

Kivimaki M, Leino-Arjas P, Virtanen M, Elovainio M, Keltikangas-Jarvinen L, Puttonen S, Vartia M, Brunner E, Vahtera J. Work stress and incidence of newly diagnosed fibromyalgia. *Journal of Psychosomatic Research.* 2004, 57: 417-422.

Klossika I, Flor H, Kamping S, et. al. Emotional modulation of pain: A clinical perspective. *Pain.* 2006, 124: 264-268.

Lacourse MG, Orr EL, Cramer SC, Cohen MJ. Brain activation during execution and motor imagery of novel and skilled sequential hand movements. *Neuroimage.* 2005, 27: 505-19.

LeDoux J. *The Emotional Brain: The mysterious underpinnings of emotional life.* Touchstone Books, Simon and Schuster, New York, NY. 1996.

Levenson RW. Autonomic nervous system differences among emotions. *Psychological Science.* 1992, 3: 23-31.

Lieberman MD, Jarcho JM, Berman S, Naliboff BD, Suyenobu BY, Mandelkern M, Mayer EA. The neural correlates of placebo effects: a disruption account. *NeuroImage.* 2004, 22: 447–455.

Lipton BH. *The Biology of Belief.* Hay House Inc., Carlsbad, CA. 2008.

MacIver K, Lloyd DM, Kelly S, Roberts N, Nurmikko T. Phantom limb pain, cortical reorganization and the therapeutic effect of mental imagery. *Brain.* 2008, 131: 2181-91.

Martin BI, Deyo RA, Mirza SK, Turner JA, Comstock BA, Hollingworth W, Sullivan SD. Expenditures and health status among adults with back and neck Problems. *Journal of the American Medical Association.* 2008, 299: 656-664.

McBeth J, Silman AJ, Gupta A, Chiu YH, Ray D, Morriss R, Dickens C, King Y, Macfarlane GJ. Moderation of psychosocial risk factors through dysfunction of the hypothalamic-pituitary-adrenal stress axis in the onset of chronic widespread musculoskeletal pain: findings of a population-based prospective cohort study. *Arthritis and Rheumatism.* 2007, 56: 360-71.

McCullough ME, Pargament KI, Thoresen CE (eds.). *Forgiveness: Theory, Research and Practice.* Guilford Press, New York, NY. 2000.

McEwen BS. Stress, adaptation, and disease: Allostasis and allostatic load. *Annals of the New York Academy of Sciences.* 1998, 840: 33-44.

Melzack R, Casey KL. Sensory, motivational and central control determinants of pain. In Kenshalo DR (ed.), *The Skin Senses.* Charles C. Thomas Publishing, Springfield, IL. 1968.

Melzack R, Coderre TJ, Vaccarino AL, Katz J. Pain and neuroplasticity. In Grafman J and Christen Y (eds.), *Neuronal plasticity: Building a bridge from the laboratory to the clinic.* Springer-Verlag Inc., Berlin, Germany. 1999.

Mitra S. Opioid-induced hyperalgesia: pathophysiology and clinical implications. *Journal of Opioid Management.* 2008, 4: 123-130.

Moseley GL, Zalucki N, Birklein F, Marinus J, van Hilten JJ, Luomajoki H. Thinking about movement hurts: the effect of motor imagery on pain and swelling in people with chronic arm pain. *Arthritis and Rheumatism.* 2008, 59: 623-31.

Ochsner KN, Zaki J, Hamelin J, Ludlow DH, Knierim K, Ramachandran T, Glover GH, Mackey SC. Your pain or mine? Common and distinct neural systems supporting the perception of pain in self and other. *Social Cognitive and Affective Neuroscience.* 2008, 3:144-160.

Ohman A. Fear and anxiety as emotional phenomena: Clinical, phenomenological, evolutionary perspectives, and information-processing mechanisms. *In Handbook of the emotions*, M. Lewis and J.M. Haviland (eds.), Guilford Press, New York, NY. 1992.

Okifuji A, Turk DC. Stress and psychophysiological dysregulation in patients with fibromyalgia syndrome. *Applied Psychophysiology and Biofeedback*. 2002, 27: 129-140.

Pennebaker J. *Writing to Heal: A guided journey to recovering from trauma and emotional upheaval*. New Harbinger Publications, Inc. Oakland, CA. 2004.

Pennebaker J. *Opening Up: The healing power of expressing emotions*. Guilford Press, New York, NY. 1990.

Peyron R, Laurent M, Garcia-Larrea, L. Functional imaging of brain responses to pain: a review and meta-analysis. *Clinical Neurophysiology*. 2000, 30: 263-288.

Ploner M, Freund HJ, Schnitzler A. Pain affect without pain sensation in a patient with a postcentral lesion. *Pain*. 1999, 81: 211-214.

Progoff I. *At a Journal Workshop: The Basic Text and Guide for Using the Intensive Journal Process*. Dialogue House Library, New York, NY. 1975

Quartana PJ, Burns JW. Painful consequences of anger suppression. *Emotion*. 2007, 7: 400-14.

Rainer T. *The new diary: How to use a journal for self guidance and expanded creativity*. Tarcher/Putnam Books, New York, NY. 1978.

Raspe H, Hueppe A, Neuhauser H. Back pain, a communicable disease? *International Journal of Epidemiology*. 2008, 37:69-74.

Rico GL. *Writing the Natural Way: Using Right-Brain Techniques to Release Your Expressive Powers*. J. P. Tarcher, Inc., Los Angeles, CA. 1983.

Roemer L, Litz BT, Orsillo SM, Ehlich PJ, Friedman MJ. Increases in Retrospective Accounts of War-Zone Exposure Over Time: The Role of PTSD Symptom Severity. *Journal of Traumatic Stress*. 1998, 11: 597-605.

Ross JS, Tkach J, Ruggieri PM, Lieber M, Lapresto E. The mind's eye: functional MR imaging evaluation of golf motor imagery. *American Journal of Neuroradiology*. 2003, 24:1036-44.

Roth G, Assor A, Niemiec CP, Deci EL. The emotional and academic consequences of parental conditional regard. *Developmental Psychology*. 2009, 45: 1119-1142.

Sarno, JE. *The Mindbody Prescription: Healing the body, healing the pain*. Warner Books, New York, NY. 1998.

Sarno JE. *The Divided Mind*. HarperCollins Books, New York, NY. 2006.

Schafe GE, Nader K, Blair HT, LeDoux JE. Memory consolidation of Pavlovian fear conditioning: a cellular and molecular perspective. *Trends in Neurosciences*. 2001, 24: 540-546.

Schmahl C, Bohus M, Esposito F, Treede RD, Di Salle F, Greffrath W, Ludaescher P, Jochims A, Lieb K, Scheffler K, Hennig J, Seifritz E. Neural correlates of antinociception in borderline personality disorder. *Archives of General Psychiatry*. 2006, 63: 659-67.

Schmitt DP, Realo A, Voracek M, Allik J. Why can't a man be more like a woman? Sex differences in big five personality traits across 55 cultures. *Journal of Personality and Social Psychology*. 2008, 94:168-182.

Schrader H, Obelieniene D, Bovim G, Surkiene D, Mickeviciene D, Miseviciene I, Sand T. Natural evolution of late whiplash syndrome outside the medicolegal context. *Lancet*. 1996, 347: 1207-11.

Schrader H, Stovner LJ, Obelieniene D, Surkiene D, Mickeviciene D, Bovim G, Sand T. Examination of the diagnostic validity of 'headache attributed to whiplash injury: a controlled, prospective study. *European Journal of Neurology*. 2006, 13: 1226-32.

Selhub, E, Infusino D. *The Love Response: Your prescription to turn off anger, fear and anxiety*. Ballantine Books, New York, NY. 2009.

Selfridge N, Peterson F. *Freedom from fibromyalgia: The 5-week program proven to conquer pain*. Three Rivers Press, New York, NY. 2001.

Sherman JJ, Turk DC, Okifuji A. Prevalence and impact of posttraumatic stress disorder-like symptoms on patients with fibromyalgia syndrome. *Clinical Journal of Pain*. 2000,16: 127-134.

Shorter, E. *From paralysis to fatigue: A history of psychosomatic illness in the modern era*. The Free Press, Simon and Schuster, New York, NY. 1992.

Siegel RD. *The mindfulness solution: Everyday practices for everyday problems*. Guilford Press, New York, NY. 2010.

Siegel RD, Urdang MH, Johnson DR. *Back sense: A revolutionary approach to halting the cycle of chronic back pain*. Broadway Books, New York, NY. 2001.

Silverman SM. Opioid induced hyperalgesia: clinical implications for the pain practitioner. *Pain Physician.* 2009, 12: 679-684.

Simotas AC, Shen T. Neck pain in demolition derby drivers. A*rchives of Physical Medicine and Rehabilitation.* 2005, 86: 693-6.

Staud R, Smitherman ML. Peripheral and central sensitization in fibromyalgia: a pathogenetic role. *Current Pain and Headache Reports.* 2002, 6: 259-266.

Stephens R, Atkins J, Kingston A. Swearing as a response to pain. *Neuroreport.* 2009, 20: 1056-1060.

Strine TW, Hootman JM. US national prevalence and correlates of low back and neck pain among adults. *Arthritis Rheumatology.* 2007, 57: 656-65.

Taddio A, Shah V, Gilbert-MacLeod C, Katz J. Conditioning and hyperalgesia in newborns exposed to repeated heel lances. *Journal of the American Medical Association.* 2002, 288: 857-61.

Taddio A, Katz J. The effects of early pain experience in neonates on pain responses in infancy and childhood. *Paediatric Drugs.* 2005, 7: 245-57.

Takamatsu H, Noda A, Murakami Y, Tatsumi M, Ichise R, Nishimura S. A PET study following treatment with a pharmacological stressor, FG7142, in conscious rhesus monkeys. *Brain Research.* 2003, 980: 275-280.

Taub E, Uswatte G, King DK, Morris D, Crago JE, Chatterjee A. A placebo-controlled trial of constraint-induced movement therapy for upper extremity after stroke. *Stroke.* 2006, 37: 1045-1049.

Trakhtenberg EC. The effects of guided imagery on the immune system: a critical review. *International Journal of Neuroscience,* 2008, 118: 839-55.

van der Kolk BA. The body keeps the score: memory and the evolving psychobiology of posttraumatic stress. *Harvard Review of Psychiatry.* 1994, 1: 253-65.

van Houdenhove B, Neerinckx E, Lysens R, Vertommen H, van Houdenhove L, Onghena P, et. al. Victimization in chronic fatigue and fibromyalgia in tertiary care: A controlled study on prevalence and characteristics. *Psychosomatics.* 2001, 42: 21-28.

Vogt BA, Sikes RW. The medial pain system, cingulated cortex, and parallel processing of nociceptive information. *Progress in Brain Research.* 2000, 122: 223-235.

Waber RL, Shiv B, Carmon Z, Ariely D. Commercial features of placebo and therapeutic efficacy. *Journal of the American Medical Association.* 2008, 299: 1016-7.

Wager TD, Rilling JK, Smith EE, Sokolik A, Casey KL, Davidson RJ, Kosslyn SM, Rose RM, Cohen JD. Placebo induced changes in fMRI in the anticipation and experience of pain. *Science.* 2004, 303: 1162-7.

Wegner, DM. *The Illusion of Conscious Will.* Bradford Books, The Massachusetts Institute of Technology Press, Cambridge, MA. 2002.

Weinstein JN, Tosteson TD, Lurie JD, Tosteson AN, Hanscom B, Skinner JS, Abdu WA, Hilibrand AS, Boden SD, Deyo RA. Surgical vs nonoperative treatment for lumbar disk herniation: the Spine Patient Outcomes Research Trial (SPORT): a randomized trial. *Journal of the American Medical Association.* 2006, 296: 2441-50.

Weinstein JN, Lurie JD, Tosteson TD, Hanscom B, Tosteson AN, Blood EA, Birkmeyer NJ, Hilibrand AS, Herkowitz H, Cammisa FP, Albert TJ, Emery SE, Lenke LG, Abdu WA, Longley M, Errico TJ, Hu SS. Surgical versus nonsurgical treatment for lumbar degenerative spondylolisthesis. *New England Journal of Medicine.* 2007, 356: 2257-70.

Westen D. The scientific status of unconscious processes: Is Freud really dead? *Journal of the American Psychoanalytic Association.* 1999, 47: 1061-1106.

Williams LE, Bargh JA. Experiencing physical warmth promotes interpersonal warmth. *Science.* 2008, 322: 606-607.

Wilson TD. *Strangers to ourselves: Discovering the adaptive unconscious.* The Belknap Press of Harvard University Press, Cambridge, MA. 2002.

Wolfe F. Fibromyalgia wars. *Journal of Rheumatology.* 2009, 36: 671-8.

Yunus MB. Fibromyalgia and overlapping disorders: the unifying concept of central sensitivity syndromes. *Seminars in Arthritis and Rheumatism.* 2007, 36: 339-56.

index

about the author

Dr. Howard Schubiner is board certified in pediatrics, adolescent medicine, and internal medicine and is the director of the Mind Body Medicine Center at Providence Hospital in Southfield, MI. He is a Clinical Professor at Wayne State University School of Medicine and is a fellow in the American College of Physicians, the American Academy of Pediatrics, and the Society for Adolescent Medicine. He has authored more than sixty publications in scientific journals and books and has given more than 250 lectures to scientific audiences regionally, nationally, and internationally. Dr. Schubiner has consulted for the American Medical Association, the National Institute on Drug Abuse, and the National Institute on Mental Health. He is also a senior teacher of mindfulness meditation. He has been included on the list of the Best Doctors in America since 2003. Dr. Schubiner lives in the Detroit area with his wife of twenty-six years and has two adult children.